Ambassador
Families

# Ambassador
# Families

## Equipping Your Kids to
## Engage Popular Culture

Mitali Perkins

**Brazos Press**
Grand Rapids, Michigan

Published by Brazos Press
a division of Baker Publishing Group
P.O. Box 6287, Grand Rapids, MI 49516-6287
www.brazospress.com

Printed in the United States of America

Library of Congress Cataloging-in-Publication Data
Perkins, Mitali.
    Ambassador families : equipping your kids to engage popular culture / Mitali Perkins.
        p.    cm.
    Includes bibliographical references.
    ISBN 1-58743-124-6 (pbk.)
    1. Parenting—Religious aspects—Christianity. 2. Popular culture—Religious aspects—Christianity. I. Title.
BV4529.P435 2005
248.8′45—dc22                                                                    2005003340

Portions of the introduction and the premise for this book originally appeared as an article in *Prism* magazine ("Training Ambassadors," *Prism*, July/August 2003).

Pages 154–156 in chapter nine, "Tenacity," originally appeared as an essay in *U.S. Catholic*, ("Not So fast," *U.S. Catholic*, July 2001).

Pages 169–171 in chapter ten, "Imagination," originally appeared as an essay in *Prism* magazine ("The Obedient Imagination," *Prism*, September/October 2002).

The map on page 24 is used by permission from The Samaritans, www.the-samaritans.com.

# Contents

# Introduction

Our ten-year-old twins had spent the past two weeks at a peaceful Christian camp. Now we were driving home, happy to be together again.

I turned in the passenger seat to feast my eyes on their faces. "If you guys have questions about anything you learned, Dad and I will try to answer them." The camp was diverse theologically, and we wondered if our boys had been drawn into any confusing debates.

But they had other things on their mind. "A kid in our cabin said he found pictures of naked people on his dad's computer," one of them announced. "Was he telling the truth?"

Rob and I exchanged glances. *Great!* I thought. *So that's what they talked about around the campfire.* "I think he might be," I said. "That's why we're so careful about the Internet."

Our other son sighed. "I can't wait to play computer games! This place was torture!" He sounded like an addict dragged into detox.

Later, we discovered that they *had* grown closer to God while enjoying the relaxed pace of life at camp. But these unexpected comments were a wake-up call about the realities of their generation's culture.

If you're anything like us, parenting these days is a perplexing vocation. Sometimes it's downright terrifying. You can almost hear the *Twilight Zone* music with Rod Serling's creepy voice saying, "You wake up after a nap. Suddenly, you're a parent on a strange planet. This is a place that showcases murder as entertainment, rewards the self-indulgence of trash-talking athletes and celebrities, promotes an addiction to accumulation, degrades sexuality as another source of cheap laughter, and chooses voyeurism over intimacy. You have entered—the world of pop culture."[1]

How do we raise kids in a society that seems to have nothing in common with the kingdom Jesus described? Sometimes we want to cloister our children away from culture's constant lure to become hooked on pleasure. At other times, we let them enjoy their generation's indulgences. ("After all, *we* turned out okay, and look what *we* did in high school.")

Books and seminars abound within Christendom warning us of the dangers facing our kids "out there." Meanwhile, the demands of busy lives (and perhaps our own resistance against legalism) result in many of us practicing *laissez-faire* parenting. But nagging doubts shred our peace. Pop culture is different now from when we were kids. It's dished up in oversized portions on MTV, ESPN, and the Internet twenty-four hours a day. It's blasted from radio stations, blazoned larger than life across billboards, trumpeted by flashy headlines at the grocery store checkout line.

How will our kids be affected if we expose them to this kind of trash? Are we failing them by not imposing rigid boundaries? Living in an era where to rebel against the previous generation is an established rite of passage, how can we glean help from an ancient book written in a Middle Eastern culture where parental authority was rarely challenged?

Some biblical passages directly address the job of parenting. In Deuteronomy, for example, God's people were told to talk about the law constantly with their kids, even writing the commandments on their foreheads so that nobody could forget them (Deut. 6:4–9). In other passages, we're told to avoid exasperating or embittering our children (Eph. 6:4; Col. 3:21). The writer of the letter to the Hebrews tells us that children respect parents who discipline them (Heb. 12:9), and a proverb commands us to train them in the way they should go (Prov. 22:6).

Wise parents have followed these guidelines through the years, but Western civilization has shifted from reinforcing biblical wisdom to rejecting it to forgetting it altogether. It's much harder to apply these principles when it can seem everybody around you thinks they're irrelevant. How many of your neighbors turn to the Bible, prayer, or the church for advice on child rearing? When problems and difficulties arise in this difficult vocation, parents in Western culture turn first to the schools, psychologists, or even celebrities before heading to the church or to the Bible for guidance. Many shudder as they imagine a stern religious figure advising them to apply the rod—or volunteering to wield it on their behalf.

The good news is that the Bible does provide wisdom designed for twenty-first-century parents living in a world with no awareness of the help God longs to provide. The question is whether we're willing to accept another challenging job—the call to become ambassador families.

## Ambassadors for Christ

In his letters to the churches at Corinth and Ephesus, two diverse, international port cities in the first century, the apostle Paul took on this job title:

We are therefore Christ's ambassadors, as though God were making his appeal through us. We implore you on Christ's behalf: Be reconciled to God. (2 Cor. 5:20)

Pray also for me, that whenever I open my mouth, words may be given me so that I will fearlessly make known the mystery of the gospel, for which I am an ambassador in chains. Pray that I may declare it fearlessly, as I should. (Eph. 6:19–20)

As parents, we're not only required to emulate Paul and become ambassadors ourselves. We're also responsible to train a new crop of ambassadors who will be effective in their generation.

What do ambassadors do? When our family lived overseas in Dhaka, Bangladesh, the American ambassador hosted an annual holiday party for Americans living in that city. We'd walk into his spacious home, and everything—the food, the furniture, the music, the conversation—reminded us of life back in the States. A great longing would overcome us for our homeland, and we'd leave reluctantly at the end of the evening. In his day-to-day life, however, the ambassador didn't stay huddled inside, gloating over his American lifestyle. He ventured daily into a restricted Muslim culture, trying to make a difference on behalf of his home country. While his loyalty to the Stars and Stripes never wavered, his effectiveness as an ambassador increased the more he spoke the language and understood the culture of Bangladesh.

During the fall of Saigon in 1975, Ambassador Graham Martin experienced the ultimate nightmare for an ambassador—fleeing from the U.S. Embassy after a humiliating loss in a costly war. He packed his bags and sent the following message to headquarters in the United States before destroying his papers:

FLASH MARTIN TO SCOWCROFT. PLAN TO CLOSE
MISSION AT ABOUT 0430 30 APRIL LOCAL TIME.
DUE TO NECESSITY TO DESTROY COMMO
GEAR, THIS IS LAST MESSAGE FROM EMBASSY
SAIGON.

Dirck Halstead, a photojournalist working for Time/Life
Corporation that day, remembers seeing the ambassador:

> I notice a lonely figure standing by the door to whom no one is
> paying any attention. I recognize Graham Martin, and everybody
> rushes toward him, pushing mikes in his face. The Ambassador
> looks sick—which he is. He has been suffering from the flu and
> exhaustion. He finally had to be physically carried out of his
> office to the waiting helicopter on the roof of the embassy, as
> the Marine security detail tossed gas grenades down the stairs
> to stem the rush of Vietnamese attempting to get out on the
> last helicopter. Everybody screams questions at the Ambassador,
> but he just turns and walks silently down a passageway into the
> bowels of the ship.[2]

Ambassador Martin's famous quote about America's military
involvement in Vietnam is curt: "In the end, we simply cut and
ran."[3] Sadly, he's often cited as an example of poor diplomacy.
But doesn't his narrow escape remind you of the church fleeing
from the world of pop culture? We've fought the wrong battles;
we've made the wrong allies; we've misunderstood the strengths
and weaknesses of the host culture. Exhausted and defeated,
drawn into "culture wars" we weren't equipped to fight, we're
fleeing as diplomatic failures.

It's time to turn around. As ambassador families for Christ,
our home country is the kingdom of God. We identify thoroughly with the customs, values, and policies of this unseen
monarchy. Yet we also seek to understand the place where
we're temporarily posted—a place that's as foreign and challenging as Vietnam was to Americans, if not more so. Our

call as ambassadors is to further the purposes of our King in the world of pop culture. Our call as parents is to train the foreign service recruits under our management—our children.

The great news is that Jesus also led his "children" into a questionable world. To his band of Jewish disciples, Samaritan society seemed as vile as pop culture sometimes seems to us. They were used to steering clear of it in order to avoid being contaminated. But their new leader deliberately interacted with Samaria. He made sure to bring them along, helping them to see God at work there, and believing they would eventually make a difference in that culture. Imitating our King, we, too, can lead our own "disciples" boldly into pop culture, hoping that our faithful presence will transform it for his sake.

Will our children want to represent the kingdom of God in their generation's version of Samaria? We're inviting them to participate in one of the most dangerous but fulfilling vocations on the planet. "I've had one of the most exciting lives anybody could possibly want," says Laura Clerici, U.S. consul-general in Mexico City. "I've been held up by bandits, I've had really bad guys after me in both Poland and Honduras. I've been part of history, and I've made a real difference in people's lives."[4] The risks and rewards are magnified a hundredfold when you represent the King of the universe.

When the best diplomats receive the call to serve their countries, they respond with a servant's heart. "You could have asked me to do anything—wash windows, sweep floors, [or] park cars," says Maura Harty, U.S. Assistant Secretary of State for Consular Affairs. "I'm still in the school of 'put me in, coach,' whatever it is my government asks me to do."[5] We pray for such an eager response to the call in the next generation of ambassadors for the King.

## Using This Book as a Travel Guide

I wrote this book to serve as a handbook for ambassador families. The first section's six chapters describe the diplomatic strategy of the King we represent. Jesus took his own "family" through Samaria to train them for their future role, and section one of *Ambassador Families* seeks to glean lessons from his border crossings. He went there deliberately, even though he faced hostility. He sought the familiar in strange places, pursued outsiders, spoke their language, and was even judged as one of the natives. Section two's four chapters describe some qualities that enable an ambassador to excel in his or her calling: patriotism, *savoir-faire*, tenacity, and last but not least, imagination.

As ambassadors of Jesus Christ to the world of popular culture, we have two vital tasks: to transform popular culture itself and to offer citizenship in the kingdom of heaven to the people we meet while journeying there. We may dispute the prioritization of these tasks, but history reveals that followers of Jesus should and indeed already have attempted both of them. Our mission hasn't changed. We're called to promote the reconciliation, justice, and healing of individuals, communities, societies, planet Earth—extending the reconciling influence of our King "to infinity and beyond," as Buzz Lightyear of Pixar's *Toy Story* declared. *Ambassador Families* explores our diplomatic efforts to individuals as well as to the culture created and sustained by those individuals.

Another goal of *Ambassador Families* is to provide a way for you to explore your family's particular call to represent Jesus in a foreign place. You won't find a list of rules and regulations in the pages to come detailing where to draw the line when it comes to your kids' involvement in pop culture. Instead, I hope to equip you to begin asking questions, to practice discernment, and to apply certain principles in the context of your own family's foreign service assignment. Foreign service can't be boiled down to a ten-step process that works universally in every host country. This book's intention is to train you to think like an ambassador so that you and your family can innovate the best diplomatic strategy for your situation.

Finally, *Ambassador Families* was written to foster discussion and reflection in community. Although I don't provide easy answers, I hope to inspire you to have life-changing conversations with one another. At the end of each chapter, a focus story and questions provide a venue for parents and kids to reflect, articulate, and pray. Here's where *Ambassador Families* gets practical, confronting the realities of movies, public schools, music, celebrities, the Internet, style, materialism, sports, television, and books. The focus story features a snapshot of a family facing a quandary in one of these cultural arenas. Their specific situation may or may not follow directly from the chapter preceding it, but the principles presented in all the chapters should equip you to discuss their dilemmas. Leaders of small groups using this book may prepare by reading the focus stories and choosing the questions they feel are most relevant to their families or groups.

A prerequisite for these types of conversations is intimacy in relationship. I recommend journeying with your kids into the world of pop culture when they are preteens. Most young kids are willing to talk with their parents openly, and you can begin to lay a foundation of respect, trust, and truth. But if you're in the painful situation where your child or teenager doesn't want your company when journeying through culture, there's still hope. God is the architect of reconciliation and the restorer of damaged relationships. Confess the struggle to a friend or two and ask for prayer. Seek the help of a trained counselor. Resources such as Focus on the Family's "Troubled With" website also provide suggestions on restoring trust and intimacy between parents and teens.[6]

As healing begins in the relationship, I encourage you to keep praying, and when the time is right, invite your teen to join conversations spurred by the questions in this book. They are designed to make kids feel like equal players, and for both parents and kids to take risks in being truthful. Make a few ground rules clear during your first meeting, whether you're with family or with a small group that includes other parents and teens. First, everything shared in conversation should be in confidence, and therefore not repeated to anybody outside the group. Second, this is not a time to give advice or to "fix" and "improve" other members in the group (we parents must particularly remember this rule). And third, anyone can plead the Fifth and pass on a question if it makes him or her uncomfortable.

From the start, I felt hesitant to write this book because our boys are by no means "finished products." I'm still in the thick of journeying with my kids through pop culture, and I never experienced a guided tour myself. If a book on parenting and popular culture is needed, shouldn't it be authored by a sage who was raised by Christian parents and/or has already raised dynamic, committed, creative children? Thankfully, there are many such excellent books that I consume voraciously (and recommend in the appendix to this book, as well as on www. ambassadorfamilies.com).

So what can *I* add? First, since the call to serve as ambassadors in pop culture is a cross-cultural one, I hope to provide a few insights gained from a lifetime of crossing borders. I lived as a child in India, Ghana, Cameroon, England, and Mexico, immigrated with my family to the United States, and became a follower of Jesus while studying at Stanford University. I spent a year doing graduate studies in India while completing my master's in public policy at the University of California–Berkeley. Since then, I've been a visiting professor of international relations at Pepperdine University, worked for several years with World Vision International as a writer and editor, and served as a missionary with the Presbyterian

Church (USA) along with my husband in India, Bangladesh, and Thailand. We now reside in Massachusetts, where I write novels for young adults and articles for various periodicals, and continue to be involved with international students and mission work.

Second, I offer you my company in this often-perplexing assignment. Again, my goal is not to provide easy answers and detailed instructions, but to explore how to make our shared dream come true—raising children who are equipped to transform pop culture instead of watching helplessly as they're captured and molded by the mores of the day. My prayer is that God will multiply the contribution of this book like bread and fish, and nourish a new generation of ambassadors for Jesus Christ.

# The First Ambassador Family

# 1

## Following Jesus into Uncharted Territory

Let us never negotiate out of fear.
But let us never fear to negotiate.

John Fitzgerald Kennedy[1]

I was twelve years old when I saw my first movie. Imagine a family of five Hindus—two parents and three teenagers—ducking into a theater on a rainy Saturday afternoon. The film was the story of a bearded white guy who divides an ocean, climbs a mountain, and smashes a couple of stone tablets into smithereens. Devoid of any Judeo-Christian background, the five of us walked out of *The Ten Commandments* scratching our heads.

It didn't take long, however, to be captivated by the experience of watching films. It was part of the process of becoming an American. The dimming of lights, the big music as the production companies announce their proprietorship—today, these cues herald the joyful, relaxing experience of sitting back while expert entertainers draw me into their story.

Movies are a powerful storytelling and moneymaking vehicle. Hollywood bigwigs know they're worth the investment, and spend outrageous amounts of money to amuse us. (At this writing, the current amount of money spent to create the most expensive film in Hollywood is greater than each of the annual budgets of fifty different countries.) Unfortunately, most moviemakers seem as unfamiliar with Judeo-Christian teachings as a Hindu immigrant watching Charlton Heston play the role of Moses. As a result, the realm of blockbuster films, full of titillating violence and spellbinding sexuality, seems intimidating and overwhelming to concerned parents. The movie industry raises a question about uncharted territory in pop culture: Doesn't it make sense to keep our children from traveling there?

## Four Types of Travelers

I've been a nomad all my life. My parents left Calcutta, India, six months after I was born. I've lived in Ghana, Cameroon, England, Mexico (where we saw *The Ten Commandments*), the West Coast of the United States, back in India, Bangladesh, Thailand, and now the East Coast of the United States. I've traveled to Switzerland, Norway, Austria, Italy, Hungary, Russia, Japan, South Korea, China, and the Philippines. When I hear the hum and buzz in airports or push through crowded train platforms, a part of me murmurs, "Ah! There's no place like home."

Through all of this journeying, I've learned that there are four kinds of people who cross cultures willingly. Some go as immigrants to embrace permanent residency in another country. Others go as the quintessential "ugly tourists," taking quick and thoughtless trips before returning with relief to the safety of known places. Still others go briefly but carefully, hoping to be transformed themselves and to leave no traces of their own culture in places they visit. The rest live overseas to make a difference in foreign places, often enjoying the pleasures within those cultures, but retaining their allegiance to their home country.

Christians travel in these four ways, also. Our goal, of course, is to be ambassadors. But some of us are tourists who take brief, judgmental trips into pop culture without much thought or preparation. Others enjoy the pleasures in that world without leaving a trace of our own kingdom's values and customs. Then there are those of us who head for pop culture as immigrants. We relocate permanently, renouncing kingdom ties, becoming citizens and even patriots in a new land.

## Change of Citizenship

My Bengali parents arrived in the "Land of Opportunity" with stars in their eyes and three preteen daughters. This was their plan: their girls would pursue studies through graduate school in America, scoring top marks and winning awards right and left. When the time came to arrange our marriages, Ma and Baba planned to use their contacts back in India to find good Bengali boys of the right caste. They imagined spending their golden years dandling beautiful Bengali grandbabies on their knees while we pursued brilliant careers in medicine, engineering, or law.

Alas! Before they could catch their breath, American pop culture and the advent of adolescence dashed those plans into smithereens. Their daughters started watching *Soul Train*, wearing hot pants and puka shells, and, worst of all, spending time with American boys. My oldest sister began dating secretly. My middle sister covered our bedroom walls with

21

posters of teen pop stars. I took things even farther and openly spent time with the son of a Presbyterian minister (whose antichurch rebellion included me—a Hindu girlfriend). My parents' American dream had morphed into a nightmare.

Ma and Baba did the best they could. But because they were among the first wave of Bengali immigrants to America, they had no example of other parents who had maneuvered their way safely through the minefields of Western culture. They had neither the energy nor the resources to develop a strategy that might include Bengali language schools, frequent trips to India, Indian-American clubs and camps. Naively, perhaps, they believed they could cocoon us away from outside influences—that we'd be shaped wholly by their Bengali values and turn out as sweet-voiced and submissive as the cousins growing up in Calcutta. (Ironically, when I became a follower of Jesus during my junior year at Stanford, my values dramatically changed. Many of my views on morals and ethics began to coincide more with my Hindu parents' way of thinking than with the mores of my secular classmates.)

Through those turbulent teen years, my parents were taken aback and shocked by the people we were becoming. We didn't want much to do with their customs and were embarrassed by any public display of "Bengali-ness." Intergenerational battles raged over clothes, music, friends, and school, intensified by the cultural divide. This warfare wore Ma and Baba out, and we began keeping secrets to protect both ourselves *and* our parents.

## "Christian" Kids Who Immigrate

As followers of Jesus, we have to face the realities of parenting, just as my parents did. First, we're not going to be able to cocoon our kids and keep them safe from popular culture, no matter how distasteful it seems to us. Second, we won't be able to cut and paste our own experiences of growing up into the documents of their lives, raising "retro-kids" who are more like the Brady Bunch than we were. This generation's world of pop culture is completely different from the place we grew up. Like Aladdin extending a hand to the Princess Jasmine in the Disney movie, pop culture invites kids to leave their parents' palace behind and discover a "whole new world."

The irony is that if we try to barricade our kids from every influence of their generation's culture, they're likely to settle there as immigrants. They may decide to carve out a new life in that other world and leave the kingdom behind. The movie *Thirteen* (2003) shocked parents with its depiction of a sweet American girl who becomes enmeshed in a world of sex and drugs. Nikki Reed, the 15-year-old who cowrote the screenplay and played the lead of Evie, told ABC News that she "simply woke up one day with a liberating thought: she would no longer care what her mother or teachers thought about her actions."[2]

Like Nikki Reed, kids raised in the church may settle into the world of pop culture, no longer caring what their parents think. Eventually, a few of them may return to their roots, but for now, they're no longer interested in kingdom citizenship. Mom and Dad's Christianity is an embarrassing legacy they try to forget as quickly as possible.

Perhaps, you, too, migrated out of the church and away from your parents' values during your teen years. "Freedom and healing have come into my life as a result of my forays out of church culture," you argue. But could you have avoided any scars or shame if your parents had helped you negotiate the pressure of life between cultures? Going places *with* your kids empowers them to travel there safely on their own, and may make a difference in their desire to retain their kingdom heritage.

23

## Purposeful Ventures into Samaria

Instead of helplessly watching our kids take up permanent citizenship in popular culture, our job is to train them to influence it on behalf of the kingdom of God. Remember, we want them to be ambassadors, not immigrants. This requires a proactive strategy of training on our part, modeled after the master. The first step is to venture boldly and purposefully into popular culture with our kids in tow.

The Gospels tell us that Jesus ventured into places others didn't expect him to go. During Jesus' lifetime, western Palestine was divided into three provinces: Judea, Samaria, and Galilee. Samaria was in the center of Palestine, but was not counted by the Jews as a part of the Holy Land.

Samaria was smack in the middle of Israel; there was no avoiding it. As the proverbial crow flies, Jerusalem was only thirty-five miles from the capital of Samaria. The high plateaus of Judea, with its steep rocky edges and difficult passes, were not as welcoming to outsiders. But Samaria's long, wide valleys, shaded by fruit trees, offered inviting roads to visi-

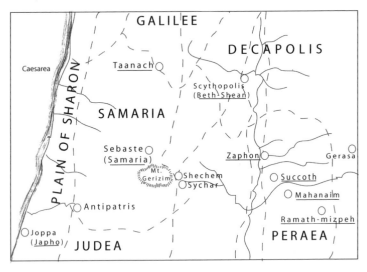

tors. Great trade routes—to the fords of the Jordan River on the east, through the cleft in the mountains at Shechem, connecting Egypt with Israel—went through Samaritan territory. People from every direction came and went, bringing their religions and traditions and leaving their imprint on Samaritan culture.

Except for the Jews, that is. Although the road through Samaria was the shortest route from Jerusalem to Galilee, pious Jews avoided it like pork. Sound familiar? Isn't this how the evangelical church has traditionally viewed the world of popular culture? Western pop culture is practically impossible to avoid, just like Samaria, even for Christians who choose to live in a separatist community. It also seems as foreign and godless a place as Samaria did to the Jews—even though in reality God may be as present and active there as inside our "safe" religious communities. As the last straw for most Christians, American pop culture comes out of a shared Judeo-Christian heritage; whether we like it or not, it's associated with our nation's historical roots in Christianity. Disconcertingly, the world of MTV, Turner, Sony, Disney, Fox, and the other entertainment epicenters of power represent Christianity to Muslims and people of other faiths. Because outsiders see the products of pop culture as the products of the Christian "church," Christians find it especially distasteful, qualifying that realm to serve as our modern-day equivalent of Jesus' Samaria.

But did Jesus cloister himself and his disciples in the familiarity of Judea? No. Although many Jews took a roundabout route on the east side of the Jordan to avoid spiritual contamination, Jesus led his disciples deliberately through Samaria on at least three recorded occasions (Luke 9:52; 17:11; John 4:4). After his resurrection, Jesus would commission them to go into "Jerusalem, Samaria, and the ends of the earth" without his physical companionship. But now, while he was with them, he led them to Samaria to prepare them for their calling.

## The Christian High Plateau

Over the past fifty years or so, much of the church has become a place that's as remote socially as Judea was geographically. If we wanted, we could stay in the high places and never descend to the plains. We could read books published only by publishers who label themselves Christian and listen to songs produced by recording companies who describe themselves as Christian. We could let our kids interact only with people who share our commitment to the "truth." We could wrinkle our noses in disgust when any mention of Samaria is heard in our fortress.

But the wide valleys and trade routes of Samaria shimmer on the horizon. Like Disney's Princess Jasmine wandering restlessly on her balcony, our kids know there's a world just beyond the railings where "no one will tell us no, or where to go."[3] Deep inside, we feel the lure, too. Once they're tucked safely in bed, many of us head for our high-resolution screens and let ourselves escape secretly. As long as we hide our trips into pop culture from our kids, we think, everything will be fine. But our kids are like Gollum pursuing the Ring when it comes to sniffing out parental hypocrisy. They'll discover it and leave us behind in disgust as they race downhill and plunge headfirst into Samaria.

The best preparation we can give them is to travel into popular culture with them, just as Jesus did with his "children."

## Vacations into Pop Culture?

One of my good friends works for Stanford University, planning incredible trips for wealthy alumni. She accompanies them to exotic destinations, stays with them in five-star hotels, and enjoys haute cuisine and first-class travel for free. But Kathy tells me that she can never relax. She's working; she's not on vacation. Fun comes with the job, but she can't forget that she's an employee. If she did, she'd be fired.

We, too, are on the job as we lead our children into the beautiful valleys of Samaria. Our main purpose is not the enjoyment or escape of tourism, but the high task of a diplomatic mission. Although we'd love to loll on the couch and channel-surf the night away, as followers of Jesus we can't indulge in that luxury. Raising ambassador kids is intertwined with the intense vocation of discipleship, and neither call can be fulfilled on autopilot.

Dick Staub, founder of the Center of Faith and Culture, writes: "After hearing my plea for cultural bridging someone will say, 'this sounds like so much work!' I could respond by quoting the late Chaim Potok who spent a life bridging his Hasidic upbringing and secular life: 'While this tension is exhausting, it is fuel for me,' Potok said. 'Without it, I would have nothing to say.'"[4]

It takes the hard work of diplomacy to have something to say.

What does a family diplomatic mission into Samaria look like? At first glance, it's not much different from a pleasure trip. We might select and watch a blockbuster movie, and then discuss it around the table, or read aloud best-selling books. It might mean listening to chart-topping albums, buying tickets to the hottest Broadway musicals (if we can afford them), or munching popcorn while tuning into popular television shows (which we might never watch if we didn't have kids).

The differences are in *how* and *why* we go.

First, when it comes to how we go, our travels with our kids require our presence and the prayerful engagement of mind, soul, heart, and strength. When someone suggests a film for our family movie night, for example, I take a few minutes to visit one or more free Web sites. Not all of these sites come from a Christian perspective, but all of them offer a "family-friendly" look at movies and media. At the time of this writing, my choices are:

- Plugged In (pluggedinonline.com), from Focus on the Family, helps you and your children make wise choices not only about movies, but music and TV too.
- U.S. Conference of Catholic Bishops Movie Reviews (usccb.org/movies/) features short, ad-free takes on thousands of films.
- Rotten Tomatoes Family Values (rottentomatoes.com/source-175) features reviews for parents from H. Arthur Taussig. (Also check out his ad-free site, filmvalues.com.)
- Movie Mom (moviemom.com) gives detailed reviews from Nell Minnow, a mom who has appeared on numerous radio and TV shows to discuss children and media.
- Michael Elliot's Christian Critic (christiancritic.com) provides discussion questions about popular movies for you to use during family devotions.
- The Christian Spotlight on Entertainment (Christian-Answers.Net) takes a wide look at pop culture, discussing everything from computer games to music to movies.
- Grading the Movies (gradingthemovies.com) reviews movies, videos, games, and music for parents.
- Screenit! Family Movie Reviews (screenit.com) lists specific details about violence, sex, profanity, and other objectionable material.

The reviewers sometimes disagree, so I usually read at least two reviews to get a fuller picture. But even a quick look on one site provides insight on how a movie measures up to the standards of truth, nobility, purity, loveliness, and excellence set out in Philippians 4:8–9.

Even when a movie seems "safe," we still need to exert the effort of discernment as we watch it. Denis Haack of Ransom Fellowship suggests that we ask the following questions in order to watch movies with discernment:

1. What was your initial or immediate reaction to the film? Why do you think you reacted that way? What was it in the film that prompted that reaction?

2. What is the message(s) of the film, or view of life and the world that is presented in the story as it unfolds? Consider how the film addresses themes such as: the nature of reality or what is really real; what's wrong with the world, and what's the solution; the fragmentation of life in our busy, pluralistic world; the significance and meaning of relationships and love; the significance and meaning of being human; whether there is right and wrong, and how we determine it; the meaning of life and history; and what happens at death.

3. What is attractive here? To whom? How is it made attractive?

4. Where do you agree? Where do you disagree? Why? In the areas in which we might disagree, how can we talk about and demonstrate the truth in a winsome and creative way in our pluralistic culture?

5. In what ways were the techniques of film-making (casting, direction, script, music, sets, action, cinematography, lighting, editing, etc.) used to get the film's message(s) across, or to make the message plausible or compelling? In what ways were they ineffective or misused?

6. Most stories actually are improvisations on a few basic motifs or story lines common to literature. What other films come to mind as you reflect on this movie? What novels or short stories? What Scriptures?[5]

With imagination, such questions can be simplified and streamlined to use with kids and teens, even in short conversations that take place on the go. Discussions like these develop the habit of "practicing the presence of God"[6] and train our children to do the same.

*Why* we go into the realm of pop culture is clearly stated in the Lord's Prayer: "Thy Kingdom come, Thy will be done in earth, as it is in Heaven" (Matt. 6:10 KJV). We head to Samaria so that God can change things there. The good news is that, like my friend Kathy on her alumni adventures, we are allowed to have fun there, too. There are pleasures at his right hand, God promises. But following Jesus means puffing uphill around the curves, not strolling down with the rest of the pleasure-seeking crowd. We're not hedonists or Epicureans—when the bountiful pleasures come, they are incidental. Fun is a gift, not our primary purpose in life. That, too, our children learn, as we lead them into Samaria not as tourists or immigrants, but as ambassadors of the King—even in the sometimes frightening, sometimes thrilling venue of film.

### Focus Story: Movies

Sylvia's kids were at her again.

"All the other fourth-graders watch PG-13 movies!" That was Jenna, hands on hips, looking mad.

Matthew's tone was more diplomatic. "Everybody in middle school's seen *Crime Fighters* except me, Mom. Even kids in youth group at church."

Sylvia sighed. She was exhausted after a long week of work, and she didn't have the energy to stand her ground in this recurring Friday-night discussion. "The rule in this house is that you don't watch a PG movie alone," she said for what felt like the hundredth time. "You don't watch a PG-

13 movie until you're thirteen." *I sound like a recording*, she thought. *Press the pound sign if you want to hear this message again. BEEP!*

"But you let us watch *Star Wars* alone once," Jenna said. "That's rated PG."

"Yeah," Matthew added. "When you had that party, remember?"

"You'd already seen that once, with me."

Sylvia held her breath. Maybe she'd escape early for once. But Matthew wasn't done: "Mom, you say that nobody should rule us except Jesus, right?"

*Good*, Sylvia thought. *He's finally getting it.* "I do say that, Matthew."

"Then why do you let a few people in Hollywood be your bosses?"

"WHAT? I do not."

"You do, Mom. The guys who rate movies are ruling you. That's who decides what movies we get to watch in this family."

Sylvia was silent. In a way, her son was right. She was beginning to feel like the ratings system was working against her, anyway. Her fourth-grader scorned all "G" movies. Her seventh-grader wanted to see every PG-13 action-adventure flick that came out, regardless of quality or content. Was the ratings system really set up for her as a parent? Or was it a way for kids to judge the "cool factor" of a movie? If she couldn't use ratings as a way to set guidelines for viewing in their home, what could she use?

**Put It into Practice**

1. What would you do if you were Sylvia? Would you let Matthew see *Crime Fighters* (rated PG-13) with his youth group at church? Why or why not?

31

2. When and why did Jesus lead his disciples into Samaria? Imagine some of the disciples' different reactions when he suggested these visits.

3. How did your parents interact with popular culture? Did they stay aloof? Did you ever catch them secretly enjoying popular culture even as they spoke out against it? Or did they travel there openly as tourists along with the rest of society? What effect did pop culture have on them? How did they transform their generation's world?

4. What does your current nuclear family do for fun? Do you relax separately or together? Does someone plan these events, or do they happen spontaneously?

5. Using Denis Haack's questions above, write a paragraph or two about a recent movie you've seen.


## Bringing It Home (for the Family or Small Group)

6. Parents: Name a couple of movies you'd let your kids watch alone. Why these two? Kids: Name a couple of movies your parents would let you watch alone. Compare and discuss your answers.

7. Parents: Have you ever turned off a movie because of unforeseen objectionable content? Kids: Have you ever felt uncomfortable or scared during a movie? Why or why not?

8. How do you decide which movies to watch as a family? Write your answers on slips of paper and then read them aloud. Discuss any differences.

9. Parents: Do the Motion Picture Association of America's (MPAA) ratings work for or against you as a parent? Name a PG-13 movie you might allow someone younger than thirteen to watch. Why? Kids: What do you think about movie ratings? Name a "G-rated" movie that you loved and would watch again.

10. Parents: Would you watch a movie that you wouldn't let your kids watch? Why or why not? Kids: How do you feel if your parents watch a PG-13 or R-rated movie that they won't let you watch? Do you think it's right for them to watch it when you can't? Why or why not?
11. Discuss a movie you watched recently using a few of Denis Haack's questions outlined in this chapter.

# 2

## Following Jesus
## into Hostile Places

All war represents a failure of diplomacy.

Tony Benn[1]

The parent of another child visited my son's class and invited
the kids to wash a statue of the Hindu elephant god. The
principal highlighted this parent-led multicultural event in the
school paper. My son's social studies teacher shared about his
lifestyle as a homosexual. The principal staunchly supported
his right to free speech. But when I asked permission to share
about how our family celebrates Easter, the answer was no.
"Mel Gibson's movie [*The Passion of the Christ*] has stirred up
too much controversy this year," I was told.

Apparently, grown-ups are entitled to free speech in the classroom if they share about Hinduism or homosexuality, but not if they want to talk about Jesus.

Hostility. Fear. Suspicion. These days, that's what you often encounter if you mention the name of Jesus without using it as an expletive. Especially in the public arena. James Dobson, the head of Focus on the Family, made national headlines when he told Christian parents in California to flee from public education. "In the state of California . . . I wouldn't put [a] youngster in a public school," Dobson announced on his radio show.[2] Five million listeners heard his advice; many parents followed it.

But most public schools are havens compared to other hazardous places we send our kids. Young people wander through the Internet alone, vulnerable to predators who stalk those streets or images that traumatize them for years. We drop them off at malls, encouraging the worship of that great idol of Western civilization, materialism. We pay money to music companies who inscribe foul lyrics into their memories. We give our kids access to cable television, where a degraded view of sexuality stunts their hearts, minds, and souls. We buy them electronic games where they are rewarded for terrible deeds like robbery or murder.

Pop culture can be a dangerous place. We'd be naïve to think otherwise before we accept the assignment of serving as family ambassadors there. In extreme cases, it can even lead to death. (Suicide is the sixth leading cause of death for 5- to 14-year-olds in the United States; it's the second leading cause among 15- to 19-year-olds.)[3]

Even if they're not killing themselves, some of our depressed and desperate daughters are starving and cutting themselves. "Something like one in every 200 adolescent girls between the ages of 13 and 19 regularly cut themselves," says Dr. Charles Goodstein, clinical associate professor of psychiatry at New York University School of Medicine. "They feel numb, so out of touch that somehow the slicing sort of validates them. It helps them release overwhelming tension—tension that stems from intense feelings that can't be communicated."[4]

Boys are not exempt from self-destruction. They're bombarded with messages that define masculinity as a mandate for destruction instead of strength and protection. *Grand Theft Auto: Vice City*, described by Amazon.com as "the undisputed best-selling video game of 2002," is rated "M" for Mature, but manufacturers target teen boys in their advertising.[5] Two stepbrothers in Tennessee, aged fourteen and sixteen, killed one driver and wounded another, claiming their shooting spree was inspired by *Grand Theft Auto*. A group of teenage boys in Oakland, California, who committed five murders, told police that before their random killing spree, they'd played hours of violent video games, including *Grand Theft Auto*. Surprised? After reading this review, you won't be:

Side missions include gunning down gang members with an Uzi, intimidating jurors by beating them with a hammer, and trying to kill a pizza delivery boy. . . . The beatings are intense and the number of weapons available is staggering. You can use a baseball bat, screwdriver, machete, or even a chainsaw to attack pedestrians to get small amounts of cash. As you attack and beat innocents, blood sprays the concrete. If you wound your victim and they try to run, you can chase them by following the blood trail. You can also get quick money by hitting people with your car. . . . One of the most notable parts (is your) ability to pick up prostitutes, drive to a secluded location, do the deed, then beat the prostitute after she gets out of the car to get your money back. . . . After you drive to a safe place, and as the car rocks back and forth, dialogue between the prostitute and the character can be heard ("Oh, yeah baby," "Make yourself at home," and "You in me yet?").[6]

If you still think that old-fashioned types overstate the dangers of pop culture, consider the sexual exploitation of children. Recently London School of Economics researchers found that nine out of ten children aged between eight and sixteen have seen pornography on the Internet. Porn sites commonly use the brand names Barbie and Disney in hidden code to ensure they crop up in general searches.[7] Our children are not only viewing pornography—they star in it. Police in the United Kingdom, for example, identified 6,500 Britons on one day who used their credit cards to buy child pornography images from a U.S. Web site.[8]

I don't know about you, but news like this makes me want to weep, rant, and rave. I understand why the disciples asked Jesus if God could rain fire and brimstone over Samaria:

> And he sent messengers on ahead. They went into a Samaritan village to get things ready for him, but the people there did not welcome him, because he was heading for Jerusalem. When the disciples James and John saw this, they asked, "Lord, do you want us to call fire down from heaven to destroy them?" But Jesus turned and rebuked them, and they went to another village. (Luke 9:52–56)

Jesus said, "If anyone causes one of these little ones who believe in me to sin, it would be better for him to be thrown into the sea with a large millstone tied around his neck" (Mark 9:42). When I see what some people involved with pop culture do to kids, I feel like tying a millstone or two around their slimy necks.

## Jesus in Unreceptive Places

How did Jesus respond to a hostile Samaria? They were as unreceptive to his presence as pop culture seems to be today.

38

Hospitality is an essential value in Middle Eastern and South Asian traditional cultures. As a grad student, I did research in the slums of Calcutta, interviewing Muslim women who scavenged for bent nails, banged them straight, and sold them to a local nail factory. Inevitably, when a woman like this heard I was coming to visit, she'd drop everything. She'd brew a fresh pot of creamy tea, and send her oldest son to spend a week of her wages on sweets. She'd borrow a chair from a more prosperous neighbor, sweep it clean, and arm two of her daughters with newspapers to fan me.

To shut the doors on a foreign visitor's face in the Middle East or South Asia is a grievous act of dishonor and rejection. Why, then, did the Samaritans, who had previously received Jesus with this type of warm welcome, close their homes to him? Their audacious behavior had one cause—Jesus was heading to Jerusalem. The Samaritans had hated Jerusalem for centuries. When the temple at Jerusalem was being rebuilt during the time of Nehemiah, they offered to help, but their offer was rejected. In retaliation, they not only tried to prevent the rebuilding of the temple and the city walls, but also built a temple themselves on Mount Gerazim near Shechem. This is where they worshipped.

The Jews, in turn, didn't allow Samaritans to sacrifice in the temple at Jerusalem. They considered marriages between Samaritans and Jews illegal. Samaria was seen as a disgusting, despicable place—in fact, a Jewish parent might have felt the same repugnance for Samaria that we might feel toward pop culture. And yet that's where Jesus led his disciples on the way to the cross.

When the Samaritans dishonored their master, who had just been transfigured and celebrated with the likes of Moses and Elijah, James and John were furious. (It's revealing that Jesus had nicknamed these brothers the "Sons of Thunder.")

Well-versed in their biblical history, they wanted a sequel to the Elijah-Ahaziah action-adventure extravaganza.

Who was Ahaziah? We find out in the Old Testament book of 1 Kings:

> Ahaziah son of Ahab became king of Israel in Samaria in the seventeenth year of Jehoshaphat king of Judah, and he reigned over Israel two years. He did evil in the eyes of the LORD, because he walked in the ways of his father and mother and in the ways of Jeroboam son of Nebat, who caused Israel to sin. He served and worshiped Baal and provoked the LORD, the God of Israel, to anger, just as his father had done. (1 Kings 22:51–53)

Ahaziah, a poster child for the enemies of God, fell through the lattice in his room from the second story and was severely injured. He sent messengers from Samaria to ask Baal-Zebub, the god of Ekron, whether he was going to recover. But the prophet Elijah, obeying an angel's orders, intercepted the messengers: "Is it because there is no God in Israel that you are going off to consult Baal-Zebub, the god of Ekron? Therefore this is what the LORD says [to Ahaziah]: 'You will not leave the bed you are lying on. You will certainly die!'" (2 Kings 1:3b–4a).

Not surprisingly, Ahaziah didn't like Elijah's message. He sent a captain with fifty soldiers, but *BOOM!* Elijah called down fire from heaven that consumed them. Ahaziah sent another captain with yet another fifty men, and *POW!* Elijah again called down fire from heaven. The third captain was smart. He "fell on his knees before Elijah. 'Man of God,' he begged, 'please have respect for my life and the lives of these fifty men, your servants! See, fire has fallen from heaven and consumed the first two captains and all their men. But now have respect for my life!'" (2 Kings 1:13b–14).

This man's life was spared, but just as Elijah had predicted, Ahaziah dropped dead. *SHAZAM!* What a demonstration of

God's power over Baal! What a way to reveal that God was the God of Jerusalem and not of Samaria! No wonder James and John wanted Jesus to show his might after enduring the rejection of the Samaritans.

Quickly, Jesus rebuked his disciples, refusing the mantle of the powerful prophet Elijah. Jesus wouldn't demonstrate God's power by destroying lives, but by saving lives. His boom, pow, and shazam would happen in unseen places against the powers of darkness. Triumphant, he would predict that the disciples would offer the ultimate welcome to the hostile Samaritans: "But you will receive power when the Holy Spirit comes on you; and you will be my witnesses in Jerusalem, and in all Judea and Samaria, and to the ends of the earth" (Acts 1:8). And they would indeed head boldly into Samaria (Acts 8:14).

## From Hostility to Hospitality

While Jesus was alive, these brothers were watching him closely. When he scolded them for their condemnation instead of heaping hatred on Samaria, they caught a glimpse of how they, too, could someday venture into hostile places. Similarly, our kids scrutinize our attitudes and responses, figuring out who's worthy of rejection and who deserves hospitality.

"Get away from my children!" I snapped, pushing through the crowd.

A Bangladeshi girl with open sores on her face tried to touch the stroller. I wrenched it out of her reach. Once again, my boys were wailing. Once again, I raced to the safety of our gated yard, almost in tears myself.

After studying third world development in graduate school, I'd had big dreams about becoming a second Mother Teresa as we headed overseas. Instead, I was spending most of my time inside, keeping our twins safe. I'd decided it was impossible to help needy people and parent young children at the

41

same time. After all, Mother Teresa had been a celibate—she didn't have kids of her own to protect. Especially not from trained beggars who descended on wealthy foreigners like a pack of hungry dogs. We weren't human beings to them; we were walking dollar bills. Besides, we'd been warned not to contribute to the racket of begging, which encouraged the purposeful abuse of children sent out by money-hungry grown-ups.

One afternoon, as the four of us boarded a rickshaw, the beggars surrounded us again. "Let's go, Mom and Dad!" our son called out. "Here come those bad people!"

My husband and I rode home in silence, shocked and grieved by the words that had come out of our son's mouth. We had longed to raise compassionate children. That's partly why we'd decided to raise kids in the third world. But now one of our four-year-old sons, adept at understanding our true emotions, was echoing hatred he must have sensed in us.

Quickly, we realized that the problem with not "giving to everyone who asks of you," as Jesus commanded in the Sermon on the Mount, was that *we* were being damaged—our hearts were becoming hard and narrow. And our children's hearts were endangered also. We needed to do something drastic, even if it did mean running the risk of supporting the Bangladeshi begging racket.

My husband went to the bank and brought home a stack of two-taka notes (worth only about three U.S. pennies each). "We're going to always have these with us," he said. "And we're going to give as many away as we can every day."

We stayed in our neighborhood and avoided tourist spots where professionals targeted foreigners. After all, we weren't short-term visitors contributing to the exploitation of unknown child beggars; we were residents who could get to know our neighbors and their stories. Miraculously, our lives began to change. I found myself looking forward to our morning walks instead of dreading them. Instead of recoiling from an outstretched hand, the boys and I pounced on a chance to give away another two-taka note. Best of all, our hearts opened up again toward the Bangladeshi people.

Those two-taka notes taught us a lesson about parenting that we'll never forget. Our own "Sons of Thunder" were watching closely to see how we reacted to hostile environments. Were these "in-your-face" dirty and disease-ridden beggars of Bangladesh worthy of God's love? Here's what the disciples learned: Jesus' hospitality extended to beggars, lepers, prostitutes, and yes, even Samaritans. He didn't come to destroy the most hostile, antagonistic evildoers on the planet, but to save them.

*WHAT?!?!* Is that welcome offered to agnostics and atheists who slam doors shut against any mention of God in the public arena? It is. Is it extended to the makers of *Grand Theft Auto: Vice City?* It is. To the marketing gurus who target kids with their seductive ads? Again, yes. *To the makers of child pornography?!?!* (Gulp!) Ye-e-e-s.

I'm having a Jonah struggle against the repentance of people like this. My maternal instincts make me WANT to see wicked child-exploiting scumbags cower before my King. Send your fire, Jesus!

*Wait a minute. I can't ask that, can I?*

"You, therefore, have no excuse, you who pass judgment on someone else," Paul told the "good Christians" in Rome after describing the degraded evildoers around them (Rom. 2:1a). "Or do you show contempt for the riches of his kindness, tolerance and patience, not realizing that God's kindness leads you toward repentance?" (Rom. 2:4).

Tainted and wrecked by my own ugly thoughts and deeds, I'll have to count on the kindness of the King myself. And so will you. In the meantime, our "Sons and Daughters of Thunder" are watching.

## Diplomacy in Hostile Regimes

So how do family ambassadors handle dangerous places? We can't just shut our eyes to evil and continue business as usual. If we stay, we do so with increased security and vigilance, remembering our purpose to train our kids and exert godly influence. Sometimes, though, it might be time for a diplomat to leave. But that doesn't mean we give up on the host country.

The United States of America, a powerful regime seeking to exert influence in every corner of the planet, rarely shuts down a foreign service outpost. Of the 191 foreign countries in the world, only four—Bhutan, Cuba, North Korea, and Iran—don't have any communication at all with the United States. The American embassy in Tehran, Iran, was shut down during the 1979 hostage crisis and never reopened. American Kelly Sobczak describes a recent visit she made to the site:

> There they are, mural after mural, demonizing my country. The colors are vibrant and the artwork, in some cases, is quite good. Of course there's the ubiquitous "Down with the U.S.A," but added to that are "When the U.S. praises us, we shall mourn," and other sayings such as "United States of America After Ghods [sic] Occupier Regime (Israel) is the Most Hated State Before Our Nation" and "We Will Make America Face a Severe Defeat." Twenty-two years after the hostage crisis the embassy is now an Iranian military installation, and I can make out armed soldiers patrolling from watchtowers. . . .
>
> Up and down the avenue I stroll, running my hands along a Statue of Liberty, whose face now takes the form of a skull; a gun with the Stars and Stripes painted inside; the face of that radical revolutionary, the Ayatollah Khomeini; and an Iranian jet being blown to bits by an American bomb, killing over 250 people in 1998. In front of the main gate the embassy's insignia can still be made out, and my fingertips trace out the words "Embassy of the United States of America," long

hacked out by irate Iranians, but the letters and an eagle are still clear to the eye.[9]

Even in the face of such intense Iranian hatred, the U.S. State Department did not give up on Iran and her people. Foreign service officers know from experience that an enemy country has the tendency to grow even more dangerous once diplomatic relations are severed. Richard L. Armitage, George W. Bush's Deputy Secretary of State, recognized the need for the United States to have a presence in Iran:

> We believe we can encourage the triumph of public resolve by engaging in direct communication with the people of Iran. We are doing this through Radio Farda, which operates 24 hours a day, and Voice of America (VOA) radio and television broadcasts into Iran. VOA has recently instituted a daily Persian television news program to Iran, in addition to its two weekly television feature programs. The State Department [also] bought on-line a website in Persian. . . . An average of 3,000 people already views [it] every day. . . . The United States has no direct diplomatic presence in Iran, but we do have what we call a "virtual embassy" in the surrounding nations and beyond.[10]

The diplomatic strategy is clear: in rare cases, ambassadors retreat to safe places, but we never stop seeking to exert influence in an unfriendly realm. We never have the luxury of a job transfer. During our time on this planet, we're always ambassadors for Christ, seeking to bless and influence people in the most hostile of places.

Our diplomatic strategy in a particular realm of culture depends on the context and history of our involvement. In my sons' public school, for example, I had visited two classrooms twice each year to talk about Christmas and Easter since they'd been in the first grade. It wasn't as if I'd been rebuffed constantly; in fact, the school had been hospitable for many years in a row. When the boys were in fourth grade, I even showed their classmates how we celebrate a Tenebrae service, explaining the last seven sayings of Jesus while my sons extinguished one candle at a time in the darkened room.

Because of this history of relating to the school, I felt we'd lose ground as ambassadors if I fought tooth and nail for the right to speak to the fifth-graders at Easter. Instead, we shifted our strategy to focus on prayer. We encouraged the boys to mention the crucifixion and resurrection in their own conversations at school. We prayed for sincerity in our efforts to be gracious to their teachers, who knew that our request to speak about faith had been turned down. It was a season in our diplomatic mission to build trust; a time to communicate clearly with our King about the situation in our host country.

In other cases, parents have chosen to confront school authorities, even if it means taking legal action:

Hamadi Alston, a third grader at Augusta Street School in Irvington, New Jersey, was suspended from school and arrested for using an L-shaped piece of paper as a gun in a pretend game of "Cops and Robbers" during "free time." Hamadi and another boy ran around using the L-shaped piece of paper as a pretend gun and exclaiming "Pow! Pow!" At no point did Hamadi or his friend threaten to harm each other or anyone else. At the conclusion of the free time period, the school's resource officer approached the boys and took them to the school office for questioning. Upset by the interrogation, Hamadi began to cry. Hamadi's parents were never informed about the situation, and when his father arrived to pick him up at the end of the day he found him crying in the office. Police officers then arrived, arrested Hamadi, and held him at the police station for four hours, during which time he was not permitted to speak to his parents. Hamadi, who had no previous disciplinary record, was charged with threatening to kill other students. After two court appearances—for which Hamadi's father paid a substantial sum in legal fees—the prosecutor finally dropped the charges. The complaint was filed against the Irvington Board of Education, its superintendent, the presiding principal of the school at the time of the incident, Hamadi's teacher, the school's resource officer and the Irvington police officers who arrested Hamadi.[12]

While this case didn't involve an issue of faith, it provides a clear example of when parental intervention is needed to protect the rights of a child. When facing a decision about whether to intervene or confront, the first step is to listen to our kids describe their situation. As ambassadors of Jesus, we pray for wisdom before beginning a process of truth-and-love decision-making. How does this process work? After seeking the counsel of trusted people, a family outlines some alternative choices of response, remembering that they serve a King of both truth and love. The first choice is always "do nothing but pray like mad." But in many cases, an injustice has been committed against a family member, and the gravity of that injustice must be taken into account. If the family decides to intervene, who will be present during the confrontation? The parent? The child? Both? What will be said and who will say it? Will the truth as they see it be written or spoken?

After more prayer that leads to making a decision about confrontation, the family envisions the best-case outcomes. How might relationships involving people and God improve and justice be restored? Next, they imagine the worst-case scenario. How could relationships involving people and God degenerate and justice be further thwarted? Each member agrees to pay the costs associated with the worst-case scenario if the family decides that truth and love demand confrontation. Still praying, they carry out their decision.

Once the people in authority respond, it's time again to pray, seek wisdom, come up with alternative courses of action, and think through the best-and-worst-case outcomes in terms of truth and love. A prayerful cycle of decision-making is an important part of representing the King in pop culture, and might serve also to solidify our kids' commitment to strive for truth and love in Samaria.

## Focus Story: Schools

Ian, a senior in high school who got straight A's, was usually quiet about his faith. That's why Gary was surprised when his son told him about the Honors Biology final paper that he wanted to write.

"I want to compare the theories of intelligent design and Darwinism," Ian said. "But I need your help, Dad."

Ian and Gary read and discussed University of California–Berkeley professor Philip Johnson's *Darwin on Trial* and other books on intelligent design. They tracked the debate between Professor Johnson and Darwinian theorists. Ian spent hours crafting a careful, cogent analysis of the two theories, and Gary edited it. The two of them went out to dinner to celebrate the day Ian turned it in.

But when the teacher handed back his paper, Ian was astounded to see a big red "D" scrawled across it. "You used unreliable sources," the teacher told him. "This isn't science—it's fantasy."

Ian's biology grade for the semester plummeted to a C, damaging his overall grade point average right when he would be applying to college. Frustrated and discouraged, he borrowed a cell phone and called Gary at the office.

"I got a 'D,' Dad!" he said, his voice breaking.

Gary took a deep breath. He should have seen this coming. He fought a wave of fury at the teacher. How should he respond? Was there anything they could do? Ian was the oldest of their four kids and they weren't rich. Was it right or even possible to find a way to afford a private Christian education for the rest of their kids?

**Put It into Practice**

1. What would you do in Gary's situation? Would you confront the teacher? Outline a truth-and-love best-case outcome (described above). If the teacher refused to change the grade, would you take it to the principal? How would you talk to your son about it?

2. Are your kids in the public schools? Has it been a relatively safe or a hostile environment for them? How have you helped them express God's love in their classrooms?

3. Reflect on the motives of James and John when they asked Jesus if *they* could call down fire on the Samaritans. How does this remind you of another time these brothers are mentioned before the day of Pentecost? (Hint: See Mark 10:35.)

4. Have you ever pulled your kids completely away from an aspect of pop culture for safety's sake? If so, give an example. Did it work? How can you influence that realm from a distance?

5. I've been tempted to start a nonprofit called "Millstone Ministries." The vision statement would be to track down those who damage children and ... well, you get the picture. List some types of people who might be the targets of this fictional organization. Spend time praying for them in the spirit of Matthew 5:44.

**Bringing It Home (for the Family or Small Group)**

6. Parents: Do you talk about your faith at work? Kids: Do you talk about your faith at school? Why or why not? How would people react if and when you mention your commitment to Jesus? Compare and discuss your answers.

7. Parents: Were your own parents fearful about aspects of your generation's culture? Which ones? Were those fears justified? Kids: List three things kids in your generation do that scare your parents. Do you think your parents are right to be worried? Why or why not?

8. Are the rules in your family about pop culture more or less strict than in your friends' families? Why or why not? Write your answers on slips of paper and then read them aloud. Discuss any differences.

# 3

## Following Jesus to Hunt for Treasure

Everything ends this way in France—everything.
Weddings, christenings, duels, funerals, swindlings,
diplomatic affairs—everything is a pretext for a good
dinner.

Jean Anouilh[1]

"Turn the volume down!" I yelled up the stairs.

*Now I sound like a parent*, I thought. Overnight, it seemed, our kids and their peers had plunged headfirst into the murky pond of their generation's music. Songs with a driving beat and incomprehensible words shook the walls of our house.

I started reading lyrics and reviews of new albums, trying to find artists that we might be able to endorse. The outcome of my research was bleak. The planet of "Christian" music and the planet of "secular" music spun in different galaxies, and my kids' friends were definitely not into visiting the former. Besides, even "Christian" artists were singing about questionable subjects.

On the jacket of a recent release aimed for tweens and teens, the musician writes, "first and foremost I would like to thank my Lord and Savior Jesus Christ who has been with me through it all." She lauds her prayer partners and her church, saying that she's "grown so much spiritually and learned so much." Sounds like a safe album, right? I thought so, too, until I read lyrics like: "Used to make love for hours, turn right around and take long hot showers," or "Turn down the lights, turn down the bed, turn down these voices inside my head, lay down with me, tell me no lies, just hold me close, don't patronize."[2]

Are songs like these "Christian" just because an artist who professes Christ as Lord performs them? Does an album have to be produced by a "Christian" company to ensure that the music is "Christian" music?

But we're an ambassador family—we aren't allowed to scurry to the safety of any evangelical bastion, real or imagined. Fleeing is tempting, because as far as I can tell, most music made popular by my kids' generation promotes fornication, materialism, and violence. A recent study by the American Psychological Association, for example, found that "violent songs increased feelings of hostility without provocation or threat . . . and this effect was not the result of differences in musical style, specific performing artist, or arousal properties of the songs. Even humorous violent songs increased aggressive thoughts."[3] We're already resisting the influence of violence in the realms of gaming and movies. Now popular performers are engraving that same theme of aggression in our children's heads.

Musicians are among the most powerful shapers of society. A friend once generously gave us tickets to attend a Bruce Springsteen concert. We marveled as thousands of our peers moaned, screamed, wept, and raised their hands in worship before the "Boss." What charisma Springsteen had! What influence!

Plato and Jimi Hendrix both pontificated on a musician's enormous capacity to affect others:

> Musical training is a more potent instrument than any other, because rhythm and harmony find their way into the inward places of the soul.[4]

> Atmospheres are going to come through music, because the music is a spiritual thing of its own.... You can hypnotize people ... and when you get them at their weakest point you can preach into the subconscious what you want to say.[5]

Many musicians singing for my kids' generation are preaching a message of death and destruction. How in the world are we supposed to lead them through this particularly dangerous realm of pop culture? Is God completely absent from the current hip-hop, rap, reggae, pop, rock, and soul hits that are making CEOs of record companies rich?

## God of All Cultures

At first glance, it seemed to me that the answer is yes; the culture of "secular" music *is* completely godless. But I'd forgotten a lesson I'd learned while crossing borders—there is no such place as a godless culture.

When I first became a follower of Jesus, I left my "godless" Indian heritage behind and immersed myself in American evangelicalism. Over two decades, though, I've found myself retreating until I'm most comfortable along the border between the two worlds. I no longer worship Hindu gods nor believe in reincarnation, but aspects of Bengali culture reflect God's character in ways not emphasized by the evangelical church. The honoring of older people, the love of lyrical poetry and language, the emphasis on relationships over possessions, the high value of hospitality, the passionate expression of emotions—I don't want to leave any of these emphases behind. They are signs of a divine presence in my life and world before I'd even heard the name of Jesus Christ.

In the process of discovering God at work in Indian culture, I was eager to discover how Indian followers of Jesus Christ expressed their faith. In my pursuit of an "Indian-flavored" Christianity, I attended an Indian Christian wedding. To my surprise, the bride wore a white dress instead of a traditional red saree (Indian women wear white only if they're widowed). Nubile bridesmaids and stalwart groomsmen flanked the couple, just as they do in American weddings. (In Hindu marriage ceremonies, only elderly relatives are invited forward to offer blessings.) The Indian couple exchanged rings instead of garlands and fed each other cake instead of rice. *Are we in Indiana or India?* I wondered.

Sadly, non-Western converts and churches often imitate their Western counterparts instead of becoming redeemed versions of their true selves. Everything associated with their cultural heritage is considered ungodly or tainted, and so has to be left behind. Some of the blame must rest on the shoulders of Western missionaries like the ones caricatured in James Michener's *Hawaii* or Barbara Kingsolver's *The Poisonwood Bible*. Not many best sellers feature the scores of missionaries who know that God is already active and present in foreign cultures. Even while encouraging new believers to eschew idolatry and avoid syncretism, they look for existing values and practices to affirm and fulfill. They celebrate the Spirit-led emergence of Christ's bride adorned in contextualized beauty instead of demanding Stepford-wife-ish replicas of their own churches.

Excellent missionaries, like ambassador parents, emulate another key aspect of Jesus' strategy—using the words and deeds of people within a so-called "godless" culture to illustrate divine truths.

## Jesus and Common Grace

On two occasions in the Gospels, Jesus used "ungodly" Samaritans to teach about godly behavior. The first was in response to a test:

> But [the expert in the law] wanted to justify himself, so he asked Jesus, "And who is my neighbor?"
>
> In reply Jesus said: "A man was going down from Jerusalem to Jericho, when he fell into the hands of robbers. They stripped him of his clothes, beat him and went away, leaving him half dead. A priest happened to be going down the same road, and when he saw the man, he passed by on the other side. So too, a Levite, when he came to the place and saw him, passed by on the other side. But a Samaritan, as he traveled, came where the man was; and when he saw him, he took pity on him. He went to him and bandaged his wounds, pouring on oil and wine. Then he put the man on his own donkey, took him to an inn and took care of him. The next day he took out two silver coins and gave them to the innkeeper. 'Look after him,' he said, 'and when I return, I will reimburse you for any extra expense you may have.'
>
> "Which of these three do you think was a neighbor to the man who fell into the hands of robbers?"
>
> The expert in the law replied, "The one who had mercy on him."
>
> Jesus told him, "Go and do likewise." (Luke 10:28–37)

Test this out. Pick a chart-topping MTV star you feel troubled about when it comes to his or her influence on pop culture.

Replace the word "Samaritan" with his or her name, replace "Levite" with evangelical, and imagine Jesus telling this story to you. Your gut response is akin to what the Jewish listeners of this parable probably felt when they heard it for the first time. ("How *dare* he use a *Samaritan* to teach a lesson about *God*?!?") I'm sure the legalistic religious expert was especially outraged by Jesus' audacity in using a completely "godless" person to illustrate the second of the two great commandments.[6]

But Jesus didn't stop there. He also used a Samaritan to teach about the first and greatest commandment:

> Now on his way to Jerusalem, Jesus traveled along the border between Samaria and Galilee. As he was going into a village, ten men who had leprosy met him. They stood at a distance and called out in a loud voice, "Jesus, Master, have pity on us!"
>
> When he saw them, he said, "Go, show yourselves to the priests." And as they went, they were cleansed.
>
> One of them, when he saw he was healed, came back, praising God in a loud voice. He threw himself at Jesus' feet and thanked him—and he was a Samaritan.
>
> Jesus asked, "Were not all ten cleansed? Where are the other nine? Was no one found to return and give praise to God except this foreigner?" Then he said to him, "Rise and go; your faith has made you well." (Luke 17:11–19)

Jesus broadcasted the ex-leper's foreign citizenship even as he commended his act of praising God. We, on the other hand, often require a "Christian" credential before praising a popular artist. I was delighted, for example, when I discovered that J. K. Rowling frequents the Church of Scotland and made sure to tell my kids, but so what? Does her church attendance make her Harry Potter series more pleasing to God?

Unlike me, Jesus wasn't tempted to "Christianize" someone before using his actions as an example. Make no mistake, Jesus said, this Samaritan *was* an outsider, and *he* did the right thing.

We, too, don't have to ensure that a musician was raised in the church or has some kind of faith before lauding a lyric that might be pleasing to God. Is our faith big enough to believe that God can use the words of a "secular" rapper or hip-hopper to reveal biblical truths about sin, hope, redemption, love, grace, or mercy? As Andrew Greeley put it, "popular culture is a 'locus theologicus,' a theological place—the locale in which one may encounter God."[7]

## "That's Good, I Like That"

Remember Maltbie Babcock's hymn? "This is my Father's world. He shines in *all* that's fair." While Babcock might have been writing about nature or scenery, Richard Mouw applies the word "fair" more broadly in a book with the same title as the hymn.[8] In an interview with *Christianity Today*, he made a case for God taking pleasure in some aspects of popular culture:

> Common-grace thinking says clearly to me that God isn't exclusively focused on saving souls.[9] Obviously, I don't know whether Barry Bonds is going to end up in heaven, but I think God likes it when he sees him hit a really fine home run. And I don't know whether Tom Hanks is going to end up in heaven, but I do believe that when I take delight in a good acting performance that I'm taking delight in something that God wants me to, that God himself delights in.
>
> And so, while I care deeply about whether these people are going to be saved, my interest in them cannot be exhausted purely in soteriological [having to do with salvation] terms. I can enjoy good musical performances, good works of art, good pieces of writing, because I think God takes delight in them, because the God who called his creation good also says let there be good music and let there be good art, and on occasion looks down on the works of some unbeliever and says, "That's good; I like that."[10]

57

A key part of our job, then, within the world of pop culture, is to discern with our kids when God might be saying, "That's good; I like that." Together, we go on the hunt for signs of beauty, truth, faith, and love, obeying St. Paul's wise counsel: "Whatever is true, whatever is noble, whatever is right, whatever is pure, whatever is lovely, whatever is admirable—if anything is excellent or praiseworthy—think about such things" (Phil. 4:8). This is our diplomatic call, even in the realm of music.

The hunt for godliness seems easier in films or books. People or characters in stories often act in excellent or praiseworthy ways. How did Luke Skywalker's rejection of hatred save his father in the movie *The Return of the Jedi*? Why did Hermione cry when Ron and Harry are reconciled after a rift in their friendship in *Harry Potter and the Goblet of Fire*? What role does the encouragement of friends play in Nemo's successful return to Pixar's gorgeously animated reef in *Finding Nemo*? These examples and countless others illuminate the power of biblical truths for our children. They widen our vision of God's activity beyond the narrow confines of culture created by and for American evangelicals.

But what about the search for God's presence in this generation's music?

## Listening "Christianly"

In order to emulate Christ in the most foreign of places, we must practice what Os Guinness called "thinking Christianly."[11] John R. W. Stott defined a "Christian mind" as "a mind which has firmly grasped the basic presuppositions of Scripture and is thoroughly informed with biblical truth."[12] Steeped in biblical wisdom, we're free listen to all kinds of music boldly, ready to hear a hint of God's voice there. With a strong awareness of identity as God's beloved disciples, we'll resist the squeeze of culture's mold and be able to discern between truth and lies. J. I. Packer even argued that followers of Jesus might enjoy music more than those who listen without Christ:

> *In thy presence there is fullness of joy, in thy right hand are pleasures for evermore* (Psalm 16:11). I hold the heady doctrine that no pleasures are so frequent or intense as those of the grateful, devoted, single-minded, whole-hearted, self-denying Christian. I maintain that the delights of work and leisure, of friendship and family, of eating and mating, of arts and crafts, of playing and watching games, of finding out and making things, of helping other people, and all the other noble pleasures that life affords, are doubled for the Christian; for, as the cheerful old Puritans used to say (no, sir, that is not a misprint, nor a Freudian lapse; I mean Puritans—the real historical Puritans, as distinct from the smug sourpusses of last-century Anglo-American imagination), the Christian tastes God in all his pleasures, and this increases them, whereas for other men pleasure brings with it a sense of hollowness which reduces it.[13]

But what about taking our kids along on this posting? They haven't had as much time to be "steeped" in Scripture. Are they mature enough to enjoy pop music without being affected by immoral agendas?

Two lessons from my past encourage me as I venture with my kids into the realm of their generation's music. The first is that when they're young, we rarely send them alone—regular parental companionship is crucial.

When I was about twelve, I was belting out a hit song in the shower: "Having my ba-a-aby. What a lovely way to say how much you love me." Paul Anka's song was playing nonstop on the radio and the catchy tune engraved the words in my mind.

Leaving the bathroom, I overheard my parents talking (in Bengali, of course): "What is this 'having my baby' song?"

"Oh my goodness. Do you think she knows about what she is singing?"

Mortified, I realized how the words of the song had sounded to my parents' ears. I wasn't having anybody's baby, for goodness' sake. Why, then, was I singing about it at the top of my lungs? Thanks to the magic of listening through my parents' ears, I was confronted with the absurdity of one particular song's lyrics.

As we accompany our children into the world of "secular" music, their own hearing is sharpened. Our presence in listening to their music as they first venture into pop culture, perhaps even more than our opinions, provides clarity in their own process of discernment. This means reading the lyrics on CD jackets and tuning into their radio station in the car. It may mean banning headphones, allowing them use of the family entertainment system, and staying in the vicinity while they listen.

The second lesson is that God is already in Samaria. He knows what's out there, and is creative enough to use an "outsider's" music to communicate biblical truth.

During my high school years, I memorized lyrics by musicians like the Beatles, Cat Stevens, the Who, and of course, the Rolling Stones. Little did I know that God planned to use some of those lyrics to reveal spiritual truth. While studying overseas in Europe, in the throes of a search for spiritual truth, I visited the site in Moscow where the czar and his relatives had been brutally murdered. I'd been wrestling with the question of human suffering, but didn't consider that a diabolical, personal enemy might be playing a significant role behind the scenes.

I wandered through the opulent galleries of the Hermitage in St. Petersburg, replete with art commandeered from Hitler and the Nazis. Portrait after painting after mural depicted the suffering of Christ. One particular piece caught my eye—a rendition of Jesus agonizing in a garden. Instantly, the words to a Rolling Stones' song came to my mind. Mick Jagger sang about someone who had been around when Jesus Christ had his moments of doubt and pain. Someone who had killed the czar and his ministers while Anastasia screamed in vain. "Sympathy for the Devil," the song was titled. Suddenly, I was electrified by the possible existence of an evil tempter who delighted in human suffering—and especially in the suffering of one particular Man. While this example may sound trivial in the retelling, I know that God was powerful enough to use Mick Jagger's song in my journey of faith, just as Jesus used Samaritans to teach his disciples about loving God and neighbor.

## Focus Story: Music

Fifteen-year-old Jan was a huge fan of Lila JJ's music. She plastered her walls with Lila's posters, bought all her albums, and had saved her allowance to buy concert tickets for Lila's appearance in town.

Jan's Mom, Rachel, felt that Lila JJ's music was upbeat and positive. While the lyrics weren't explicitly about Christianity, Lila's messages about girl power, love, and friendship seemed tame enough.

But then Rachel walked in while Jan and her friends were watching one of Lila JJ's music videos. The musician was undulating on stage with three hunks. The words they were singing were about love, but Lila's dancing implied she was thinking more about sex—and wanting her audience to join her in the pursuit. At one point, Lila peeled off her blouse, revealing a lacy bra, and spun around a pole in a way that reminded Rachel of a striptease.

"Turn it off, honey," Rachel said.

"What? Why? We need to memorize the words to this new song before the concert."

*The concert!* Rachel thought. If Lila JJ was this provocative on the video, how would she behave on stage in front of a live audience? Jan's heart would be broken if she couldn't go—she'd already bought the tickets; she and her friends were going together.

Should Rachel allow Jan to attend the concert that weekend?

## Put It into Practice

1. What would you do in Rachel's situation? Would you let Jan go with her friends? Why or why not? If you decided to let her join her friends, how would you prepare her for the experience?

2. Could Rachel or Jan have done anything differently before finding herself in such a tight situation? If so, what?

3. Do you listen to Christian music? Do the lyrics alone determine if music is Christian? What about the rhythms and melodies of the music itself? Read the following statements and decide which one of them, if any, you might endorse:

   a. We hold these truths to be self-evident, that all music was created equal, that no instrument or style of music is in itself evil—that the diversity of musical expression which flows forth from man is but one evidence of the boundless creativity of our Heavenly Father.[14]

   b. Music directly represents the passions or states of the soul—gentleness, anger, courage, temperance. . . . If a person habitually listens to the kind of music that rouses ignoble passions, his whole character will be shaped to an ignoble form. In short, if one listens to the wrong kind of music he will become the wrong kind of person; but conversely, if he listens to the right kind of music he will tend to become the right kind of person.[15]

c. You cannot put the gospel to just any harmony, any beat, any rhythm. The more Christians try and be like the world, the further they will go from the true spirit of the gospel.[16]

4. As you watch movies or television, note how music without lyrics is used to convey emotions. Martin Luther said, "For whether you wish to comfort the sad, terrify the happy, encourage the despairing, humble the proud, calm the passionate, or appease those full of hate—and who could number all these masters of the human heart, namely, the emotions, inclinations, and affections that impel men to evil or good?—what more effective means than music could you find?"[17] Can music actually make you feel certain emotions or does it allow you to express emotions you are already feeling?

5. Describe something you saw or heard recently in the world of pop culture that God might affirm with a resounding "That's good; I like that." What do you think God would specifically like about the example you picked?

## Bringing It Home (for the Family or Small Group)

6. Parents: What music do you enjoy when you're alone? Kids: Would you listen to that music on your own? Why or why not?

7. Kids: What music do you enjoy when you're alone? Parents: Would you listen to that music on your own? Why or why not?

63

8. Parents: What aspects of pop culture do you wish you had avoided as a teen? Why? Kids: Does your parents' presence affect your experience of listening to music? If so, how?

9. Have you ever turned off a song that other people around you seemed to like? Why or why not?

10. Bring the jacket that contains the lyrics of your favorite album. Read the words to the songs and write down two phrases that are true, noble, right, pure, lovely, admirable, excellent, or praiseworthy on your own album. Switch jackets with someone else and do the same with that album.

11. When you have time for extended Bible study, review how singing and music is described in the Bible. (See Judg. 5:3; 2 Chron. 7:6; Pss. 27:6; 47:7; 68:25; 81:1; 87:7; 89:1; 98:5; 108:1; 144:9; 147:7; and Eph. 5:19.) Why did God create music? Prayerfully compose a brief vision statement about your own or your family's use and enjoyment of music.

# 4

## Following Jesus to
## Find the Outsider

A diplomat is a man who always
remembers a woman's birthday
but never remembers her age.

Robert Frost[1]

Let me confess to a slight case of "celebraholism."[2]

Inside the doctor's office, waiting for routine but uncomfortable examinations, leafing through *People* magazine is a silver lining in an otherwise bleak experience. Of course, if my kids or a "literary" friend caught me, I'd deny any salacious pleasure I take in reading about pop icons. "I'm putting my fingers on the pulse of pop culture," I'd insist.

But traces of the disease are there. On a visit home to the States while we were living in Thailand, we attended a church in the Los Angeles area. During the time set aside for congregants to greet one another, the woman sitting next to me smiled and said hello.

I shook her hand and introduced myself. "What's your name?" I asked.

"Tanya," she replied, looking bemused. (Names have been changed to protect the famous.)

As we drove along the 405 after church, I saw the same face on a billboard endorsing an expensive watch. Of course! With typical missionary ignorance about pop culture, I'd been sitting beside one of the top fashion icons of the day.

Then came the surprise of my own reaction. Some of it was focused on her: *Was she hurt that I hadn't recognized her? Or did she enjoy feeling anonymous in church for once?* But much of my gut response was embarrassingly adolescent: *Wow! Wait till I tell my missionary friends back in Thailand!*

The ancient Greeks said, "Tell me whom you admire and I'll tell you who you are."

Ambassadors are sometimes required by their governments to court and entertain valued citizens who are not those in power within the host country. Sometimes this means eschewing the pursuit of strongmen and visiting opposition leaders in hiding. Along the border between Thailand and Burma, for example, in the refugee camps where the Karenni people wait for freedom from an oppressive Burmese government, we met men and women who were dressed simply and living in bamboo huts. They didn't look like powerful leaders, but when they introduced themselves, they'd say things like "I'm the secretary of state" or "I'm the defense minister." If the American government had high hopes for Karenni independence, it would be in their interest to build relationships with these despised Burmese citizens.

In the same way, the powerful in the world of popular culture are not necessarily those we're called to admire or pursue. Is it more of a coup if a popular athlete or a movie star professes faith in Jesus? "Greater evangelistic impact," one might answer, but does that mean we focus time, talents, and energy to secure conversions of people who might receive more media attention?

Ambassadors for the King always have to ask ourselves a vital question: who is important to Jesus? A quick answer might be "Everybody," but a closer look at Jesus' interactions in Samaria might shed some light on kingdom priorities when it comes to people.

## Jesus and the Outcast

Jesus didn't shy away from powerless outsiders—in fact, he loved to spend time with them, and always pointedly in front of his disciples. Much to the disciples' surprise, he once engaged a Samaritan woman in intimate conversation. At the edge of the ungodly culture, he found the least likely candidate for his attention:

> The Pharisees heard that Jesus was gaining and baptizing more disciples than John, although in fact it was not Jesus who baptized, but his disciples. When the Lord learned of this, he left Judea and went back once more to Galilee.
>
> When a Samaritan woman came to draw water, Jesus said to her, "Will you give me a drink?" (His disciples had gone into the town to buy food.)
>
> The Samaritan woman said to him, "You are a Jew and I am a Samaritan woman. How can you ask me for a drink?" (For Jews do not associate with Samaritans.) (John 4:1–9)

Nor did religious teachers associate with shady women. In fact the cultural gap between Jesus and this woman is as great as the one between Rick Warren of Saddleback fame (or any other white, male evangelical leader) and Li'l Kim (substitute any other sexy female rapper). Picture the former asking the latter to borrow money for a soda, and you get a feel for Jesus' outrageous behavior. Later, we discover not only that the woman at the well is a Samaritan, but that she's also an outcast within her own culture because of promiscuity. We'll reflect on Jesus' conversation with a "sleazy" woman in the next chapter, but let's see what happens *after* their shocking tête-à-tête:

> Just then his disciples returned and were surprised to find him talking with a woman. But no one asked, "What do you want?" or "Why are you talking with her?"
>
> Then, leaving her water jar, the woman went back to the town and said to the people, "Come, see a man who told me everything I ever did. Could this be the Christ?" They came out of the town and made their way toward him.
>
> Meanwhile his disciples urged him, "Rabbi, eat something."
>
> But he said to them, "I have food to eat that you know nothing about."
>
> Then his disciples said to each other, "Could someone have brought him food?"
>
> "My food," said Jesus, "is to do the will of him who sent me and to finish his work. Do you not say, 'Four months more and then the harvest'? I tell you, open your eyes and look at the fields! They are ripe for harvest. Even now the reaper draws his wages, even now he harvests the crop for eternal life, so that the sower and the reaper may be glad together. Thus the saying 'One sows and another reaps' is true. I sent you to reap what you have not worked for. Others have done the hard work, and you have reaped the benefits of their labor."
>
> Many of the Samaritans from that town believed in him because of the woman's testimony, "He told me everything I ever did." So when the Samaritans came to him, they urged him to stay with them, and he stayed two days. And because of his words many more became believers.
>
> They said to the woman, "We no longer believe just because of what you said; now we have heard for ourselves, and we

know that this man really is the Savior of the world." (John 4:27–42)

As a result of Jesus' questionable interaction with a Samaritan woman, a whole community decides to believe that Jesus was the Messiah! What a lesson to the disciples! They would never forget how their Master's interaction with a powerless outsider transformed a village.

In the same way, our children are watching our relationships with people along the margins of culture. Do we talk to those tattooed kids at the skate park? What's our reaction as we drive past the Goth teens clustered on the corner? What about that girl dressed like a pop-queen-wannabe? How will Mom or Dad treat her, and how will they respond to the homeless guy who approaches us for a handout?

In August of 2001, when our lives seemed at a peak of bustle and rush, I reluctantly signed us up to serve as a host family through Boston University's Humphrey Fellow program. We were assigned a scholar from Jordan who had brought along his wife and two preschoolers. One month later, when 9/11 took place, I began to recognize the gift given our family.

As anger against Muslims simmered in our nation, our sons began to perceive and comment on attitudes of rigidity and hatred. After all, for them, it was personal. Our Jordanian friends described the suspicion, hostility, and prejudice they were encountering in Boston, and the boys saw tears in their eyes. Rahilah wore a traditional Muslim head scarf, and she was the epitome of sweetness and generosity. Ahmad, too, was a follower of Islam, and gentle and hospitable toward everybody he met. Besides, how could *anybody* hate toddlers who looked at you with the wide-eyed admiration usually reserved for a superhero?

We clung to that friendship throughout that year, thankful for the grace our children (and we) were given to grow in hospitality toward the "alien and stranger." As we try to love people who are completely unlike us, we hope that our kids, too, may step out in faith as fearless ambassadors into their generation's world, with a focus on the outcast as one emphasis of their diplomatic strategy.

## Jesus and Celebrities

Turning back to John's Gospel, note that Jesus and his disciples spent two full days as guests of the despised Samaritans. Immediately after this two-day Samaritan adventure, a powerful person invited Jesus to visit. This time, Jesus healed quietly and quickly from afar, choosing to play down his power in the public eye:

After the two days he left for Galilee. (Now Jesus himself had pointed out that a prophet has no honor in his own country.) When he arrived in Galilee, the Galileans welcomed him. They had seen all that he had done in Jerusalem at the Passover Feast, for they also had been there.

Once more he visited Cana in Galilee, where he had turned the water into wine. And there was a certain royal official whose son lay sick at Capernaum. When this man heard that Jesus had arrived in Galilee from Judea, he went to him and begged him to come and heal his son, who was close to death.

"Unless you people see miraculous signs and wonders," Jesus told him, "you will never believe."

The royal official said, "Sir, come down before my child dies."

Jesus replied, "You may go. Your son will live."

The man took Jesus at his word and departed. While he was still on the way, his servants met him with the news that his boy was living. When he inquired as to the time when his son got better, they said to him, "The fever left him yesterday at the seventh hour."

70

Then the father realized that this was the exact time at which Jesus had said to him, "Your son will live." So he and all his household believed.

This was the second miraculous sign that Jesus performed, having come from Judea to Galilee. (John 4:43–54)

This juxtaposition of choice—spending two days and nights in an unknown, remote corner of defiled Samaria and then refusing a royal official's invitation to perform a public healing—was no accident. Another point was being made. The disciples, like our children, watched and learned that public acclaim for an act of service wasn't valued in the King's realm.

But our King didn't leave it at that. He did hear and respond, answering the cry of this powerful man. He saw the man not as a royal official but as a suffering father, desperate with grief and longing for his son's healing. Looking beyond the power and prestige, Jesus recognized another person in need of grace.

## Inside the Cloister: A Parallel Universe of Celebraholism

Sadly, most of us in middle-class Western churches miss the mark when it comes to relating to the powerless *and* the powerful. I was reminded of our evangelical dilemma one afternoon as I drove through the narrow streets of Chiang Mai, a city nestled at the foot of the mountains in northern Thailand. The boys and I had been invited to visit a playgroup inside the compound of the American colony. A grim-looking guard checked my ID, glared through the windows at the boys, and grudgingly opened the gates.

My jaw dropped. Suddenly, we were smack in the middle of a stereotypical Midwestern suburb. Blond children skipped across lawns in front of ranch-style houses. The streets were

71

wide, paved, and smooth, with no signs of the narrow lanes and potholes that made a drive through Chiang Mai rival an exciting video game. Costco play structures, SUVs in the driveways, air conditioners whirring furiously to banish the Thai humidity. The sense of traveling into another world was so strong, I almost expected our tires to squash a host of wicked witches as we drove along.

Chiang Mai was close to the once-notorious Golden Triangle, and the American diplomatic presence there included a crowd of Drug Enforcement Agency employees and their families. A commissary assured these Americans access to their favorite food, American cars were shipped in for them to drive, and they tuned into familiar sitcoms via satellite. The gated and walled compound encircling their community provided a sense of security. With a few notable exceptions, spouses and kids who accompanied employees of the American government rarely learned Thai, and socialized mainly with one another or with other internationals.

This pseudo-American enclave in Chiang Mai was to me a metaphor of life within the church. We like to surround ourselves with replicas of ourselves. To outsiders, we feel like an exclusive fraternity who insist on a spiritualized version of "rush" before letting them in. But something's wrong when all our friends dress like us, make about as much money as we do (or more), and ascribe to the same political and moral codes. What twisted version of Christianity does this convey—especially to our children? Are we making efforts to build relationships with the kind of outcast Jesus pursued in Samaria? Or with anybody who differs significantly from us when it comes to race, socioeconomic status, religion, or culture? Our kids, too, must experience life as foreigners outside the evangelical cloister—it's the only way to develop a heart for the marginalized, the outcast, the alien, and the stranger.

Another sad trend that permeates evangelical culture is an obsession with celebrity that rivals the disease in pop culture. Powerful people are followed and adulated. Rich people are glorified and admired. Beautiful people are adored and emulated—even to the point of fans pursuing "extreme makeover" surgery to acquire *her* lips, *his* nose, *her* shape. We might not go under the knife as Christians, but we talk about celebrities and let our minds linger on the details of their lives to the point of verging on idolatry.

Writing from London, Karen Armstrong comments on the culture's shift of focus from heroism to celebrity:

> The fact that we call people "stars" is itself significant. A star sheds light in darkness. Travelers once used the constellations to help them to find the right path. We have always looked to exemplary human beings for guidance and inspiration. Throughout history, heroes and sages have become paradigmatic figures. They show us what humanity can be, they define our values, and fill us with profound emotion, because they touch an inchoate but powerful yearning for human excellence. . . .
>
> We no longer require our celebrities to go out into the wilderness to bring spiritual benefit to others. . . . We do not expect our celebrities to challenge us . . . [or] shock us out of our habitual selfishness by making us aware of the ubiquity of human suffering. We want our stars to distract us from these uncomfortable realities. . . . An increasing number of people simply want to be famous. A questionnaire recently circulated in a New York high school, asked its students: "What do you hope to be?" Two thirds replied: "A celebrity."[3]

In the parallel universe of our evangelical compound, we fawn over our own famous folk. Christian autograph hounds pursue best-selling CBA (Christian Bookseller's Association) authors and chart-topping CMA (Christian Music Association) musicians with the fervency of their secular counterparts.

The disease has permeated God's church until we no longer climb the narrow way with our King and see people clearly. Instead, we traipse along the wide road with the rest of the world, valuing fame more than the people who are concealed by it.

L'Abri's Dick Keyes defines heroes as people who excel at something we prize and inspire us to try to imitate their achievements. The difference between heroism and celebrity, according to Keyes, is that "celebrity is indifferent to moral character." Consequently, the people we admire and try to emulate reveal what *we* prize. If a person we've never met intrigues us, we must ask why we're drawn to that person. Is it her beauty? His wealth? Her power? His athletic ability? Hopefully, we're interested because he or she is someone who "show[s] qualities of moral character," as Keyes puts it.[4]

As followers of Jesus, though, we remember that even the most moral martyr or missionary is broken and damaged like the rest of us. Ultimately, what we admire is the effort of a person emulating the one true hero. The desire to be a "fan" is best expressed in the wholehearted adulation of the only person on the planet designed to receive it—Jesus of Nazareth.

## Powerful Outcasts

"Mom, you actually *liked* Michael Jackson when you were a kid?" my son asked.

"I listened to his music, honey. He seemed sweet."

"Why is he so messed up now?"

"It's hard to grow up as a celebrity. Most people get wrecked by it."

Kids at school were talking about Michael Jackson nonstop, and my son's interest in the pop star's plight verged on the obsessive. Exasperated, I kept telling him that we didn't know

Michael Jackson personally. We couldn't understand his suffering or problems, and so we neither had the right to judge nor slander him. "You should pray for him instead of talking about him behind his back," I suggested sanctimoniously.

"Good idea!"

Not so good. Our son prayed night after night for Michael Jackson, ceasing only when the recess buzz over this particular celebrity died down. *Kids are being orphaned by AIDS in Africa*, I grumbled inwardly, *and we're praying for a rich pop star every night?*

Still, there was something right about dragging the "King of Pop" before the throne of the King of Kings. It reminded us who was in charge, and how in need of mercy we all are, rich and poor, powerful and weak, outcast and celebrity. As ambassador families, we seek to transform the host culture's "celebraholism" instead of being seduced by it. We represent a King who spent leisurely time with an outcast from Samaria instead of racing to accept an invitation from a local "star." We can't, however, overlook that he healed and restored the royal official's son along with the Samaritan woman. Followers of Jesus must care about the powerful insider as well as the powerless outsider—seeing them both in need of healing.

Western culture ignores the powerless outcast and fawns over the powerful celebrity. But remember what happened to the golden calf? The worship of an idol usually leads to the destruction of that idol. Ironically, a celebrity may end up as isolated and trapped as a person on the other end of the spectrum of fame and money. Our goal is to train our children to recognize the hunger in the body of an AIDS orphan in Kenya along with the hunger in the soul of a teenager who flaunts her body for the public eye. Both suffer, to different extents and in different intensities, of course, but as ambassadors for the King, we desire restoration for both of them.

## Focus Story: Celebrity

Tara was back from the opening of a Casey Macintosh movie, her face alight with pleasure at seeing her favorite actor play the role of medieval knight.

"How was the movie, honey?" Sandra asked.

Tara's seventeen-year-old brother Kyle snorted. "That boring flick got the worst reviews. I can't believe you let her go see it. All she wants to do is salivate over that moron. God said, 'You shall have no other gods before me,' remember?"

Tara ignored her brother. "It was awesome, Mom. He was so cute. Amanda and I are going again next weekend."

Sandra frowned. Posters of Casey Macintosh lined fourteen-year-old Tara's wall. There was even a close-up of the star's face on the ceiling over Tara's bed. Tara and her friends had seen every movie featuring the twenty-something actor at least three times each, and pored over copies of *Twist* and *Teen People* to find any mention of Casey's name. Perhaps Kyle was right?

"Don't you think it's a bit much to waste your savings on the same movie again, honey? Why don't you wait for the DVD to come out?"

"It's *not* a waste, Mom. You and Dad rush us through dinner so you can hear that boring guy on NPR do his thing. And you buy every book he writes. What's the difference?"

Kyle released another "enlightened" big-brother snort. "The difference is that Casey Macintosh is a complete idiot who trashes the environment and chases anything in a short skirt."

"He does not! Mo-o-om! Make him stop!"

## Put It into Practice

1. What would you do in Sandra's situation? Why?

2. When you have time for extended Bible study, list the rich, powerful individuals with whom Jesus interacted. Now list the weak, broken, powerless people featured in a one-on-one encounter with Jesus. Tally the count. Is it surprising in any way?

3. Take out your calendar or appointment book for the past month. Note the names of everybody with whom you spent one-on-one time. Is there anyone on the list who represents a "Samaritan woman" to you?

4. Buy or borrow a copy of *People* magazine or *Entertainment Weekly.* What types of information do the editors think readers want to know about celebrities? Underline anything in the articles that reminds you of one of the nine "fruits of the Spirit" as listed in Galatians 5:22–23 ("love, joy, peace, patience, kindness, goodness, faithfulness, gentleness and self-control"). Are the editors trying to transform celebrities into heroes? Or are they attempting to show that stars are "just like us"? Which celebrity behaviors do the writers laud and which do they condemn? Discuss or write about your findings.

## Bringing It Home (for the Family or Small Group)

5. Parents and Kids: Have you ever been *very* interested in the life of a particular celebrity? Why that particular person? What attributes or character traits did you admire or prize? How did this person remind us of the ultimate hero—Jesus? Did your interest wane? When and why?

6. Discuss: Can fascination with a celebrity harm us or our faith? If so, how? If not, why not? Does the adulation of strangers harm the celebrity in any way?

7. Kids: Which of your parents' friends or acquaintances is least like your parents? How do you feel about that

relationship? Which of your friends is least like you? Is this a difficult relationship or an easy one? If you can't think of anybody in the present, consider the past.

8. Parents: Which of your child's friends or acquaintances is least like your child? How do you feel about that relationship? Which of your friends is least like you? Is this a difficult relationship or an easy one? Tell your kids about a friendship you had in middle or high school with someone completely unlike you.

9. Kids: If you could change one thing about the way your parents relate to people in your generation, what would it be? Parents: Is this change warranted? Why or why not?

10. Write a family poem comparing a celebrity and a hero.

11. Take out that *People* magazine again and choose a celebrity you find especially annoying or fascinating. Remember the friends of your parents or children you named in questions 7 and 8? Agree on a period of time during which you will pray for these people, both celebrities and outcasts, either individually or as a family. Reflect on whether prayer changes your attitude toward them.

# 5

## Following Jesus to Speak the Language

There is no diplomacy like candor.

Edward Verrall Lucas[1]

If you're an expatriate woman, Bangladesh is one of the toughest places in the world to live. It's a conservative Muslim country, so you have to cover yourself from head to toe despite the humidity and heat. Beggars besiege you, as I described earlier, and strangers treat you like a bank instead of a person. Some *bideshi* (foreign) women complain that Bangladeshi men have two ways of connecting—to cheat or to pinch. "This is a scary place," these women conclude, and retreat to the safety of the American, Australian, or European clubs. Even nonwhite foreign women feel fearful venturing out alone in the streets of Dhaka, including other Indian-born expatriates like me.

I didn't like the crowds or pollution either, but I was never frightened during the three years we lived in Bangladesh. I went alone to visit an American prisoner in jail, where incoming criminals were chained together with foot shackles and the conditions reminded me of the Turkish prison in that 1980s movie *Midnight Express*. My preschoolers and I took a nighttime boat ride along a river reputed to harbor crocodiles and bandits. In both settings, I felt safe, protected by the Bangladeshis who worked as prison guards and boatmen. Was I nuts? Reckless? (Maybe. I contracted dengue fever on the boat ride; the boys were fine.) Was I braver than other foreign women? No—anyone who knows me well recognizes the streak of caution in my psyche. I'm not bragging when I tell you about my adventures in Bangladesh. There was only one reason that I was able to venture into places that seemed dangerous to other expatriate women.

Bangla is the official language in the Indian state of West Bengal where I was born.

I speak the language.

"Bangladesh" literally means "Land of the Bangla language." Bangladeshis fought a bloody war of independence against Pakistan so that Urdu wouldn't become their official national language. Because they shed blood on behalf of it, the passion Bangladeshis have for Bangla is fierce. To succeed in Bangladesh, the best missionaries, diplomats, and development workers master Bangla—not only the spoken and written versions, but also the nuanced nonverbals like the slow head tip or the shoulder shrug.

### Our Kids: The Face of the Kingdom in Pop Culture?

"Be the Face of America to the World!" So declares the U.S. State Department's recruiting arm. In order to "be the face" of their home country, diplomats try to speak the host country's language proficiently. Foreign service employees learn one or more of sixty or so different languages in Washington, D.C., and overseas.[2] (Bangla is one of these languages.)

If our kids are to "be the face" of Jesus in the world of pop culture, we must encourage them to use and master the language of that host country. Our task as parents is not to master it (although it wouldn't hurt to be somewhat proficient), but to model and train how to use language in general for kingdom purposes.

"Yo," my son greets his friend.

"Hey."

"Hi, Evan. How are you?" I ask.

"I'm fine, Mrs. Perkins."

If I were to follow up on Evan's "Hey" with a "Yo, homee, whassup?" my son would be mortified. His friend would think I was bizarre, and any jargon I attempted would probably already be passé by the time I wielded it. If my son, on the other hand, answered his friend using the words and gestures I had used, he would sound equally strange.

Our kids' generation provides the fuel for the fast-moving train of pop culture. They speak a language unique to their generation, and communicate through nonverbal gestures we might never master. They connect face-to-face, but also via instant messaging, on cell phones, and in chat rooms. As ambassador parents, our goal is to give our kids freedom and encouragement to become fluent in the vernacular of pop culture. At the same time, we try to instill in them a desire to communicate for kingdom purposes, just as ambassadors are trained to do.

What were the purposes of our King during his diplomatic ventures into Samaria? They were always people-focused, as we want to be in any efforts to affect popular culture. In his encounter with the Samaritan woman, Jesus used the jargon of his day to connect, intrigue, know, and reveal.

## Jesus Connected by Asking for Help

The first purpose of speaking the vernacular is to *connect*. One of the best ways to connect cross-culturally is to ask for help. I learned this firsthand in Bangladesh. Expatriates told horrible (perhaps apocryphal) stories of Bangladeshi mobs attacking foreigners in stranded cars. During one of my first days of driving my children through the streets of Dhaka, I managed to lodge the car in a muddy ditch, tires whirling helplessly. I made sure the boys were secure in their car seats, turned off the engine, and stepped out. A crowd of rickshaw-pullers had already gathered. I took a deep breath and opened my mouth.

Want to see fifty Bangladeshi faces light up? Hail them with the familiar Muslim greeting: "A-salam-a-lekum." Then launch into a Bangla description of your quandary and ask for help. Two dozen rickshaw-pullers immediately climbed into the mud and heaved my car out. They wouldn't accept any payment, despite my repeated efforts, and waved us off with wide smiles.

In a poverty-stricken country where millions of dollars of aid disappear daily into the system, a foreigner rarely asks for anything from a Bangladeshi. It's as surprising a scenario as the one Jesus initiated by Jacob's well on the outskirts of a Samaritan village:

> When a Samaritan woman came to draw water, Jesus said to her, "Will you give me a drink?" (His disciples had gone into the town to buy food.)
> The Samaritan woman said to him, "You are a Jew and I am a Samaritan woman. How can you ask me for a drink?" (For Jews do not associate with Samaritans.) (John 4:7–9)

Our King understood the power of a genuine request for help in his quest for connection. He had a need (thirst) and he asked the Samaritan woman to use her resources to take care of it (water jug). What a way to break down her natural suspicion! There's nothing more disarming and less condescending than a request for help from someone you think is going to spurn you. It's like a white police officer getting out of his car in a "bad" neighborhood, finding a group of African-American young men, and asking for directions. Try it yourself—cross racial, social, economic barriers with a genuine request for help that another person can meet. I can almost guarantee surprising results.

The key is to be genuine—not contrive a request in order to manipulate for "spiritual" purposes. Our ambassadors-in-training must see *us* taking the advice of an agnostic neighbor, for example, or enjoying novels recommended by a New Age coworker. In turn, they may catch onto math because of the creativity of a Buddhist teacher, master a difficult violin piece with the help of a patient atheist, grasp the concept of teamwork from a Jewish soccer coach. We miss many gifts if we think God can teach or equip us only through people who profess faith in Jesus.

## Jesus Intrigued by Avoiding Religious Language

Trot Nixon, right fielder for the Boston Red Sox, wore a goatee and shaved his head along with many of his teammates. Unlike most of them, however, Nixon used every media opportunity to talk about God. During one televised interview, the reporter asked how Nixon had endured a time of waiting for an injury to heal.

It was tough, the athlete admitted. He went on to list some advantages of the respite from competitive play—the chance to develop friendships with younger players and extra time to read the Bible. "Besides, I know the man upstairs is in charge of my life," he said, grinning.

Nixon's choice of words probably wouldn't impress a crowd of tweedy intellectuals. But on a sunny afternoon at Fenway, he managed to strike exactly the right note for earthy, passionate Sox fans. In the back of their minds, a few might wonder: *Who does Trot mean by the "man upstairs"? Is he talking about somebody in the luxury boxes? Does he really read the Bible?*

Nixon's disarming interview illustrates the King's second purpose of communicating—to *intrigue* others about spiritual truths. Jesus approached the Samaritan woman by asking for water, but the conversation soon headed elsewhere:

> Jesus answered her, "If you knew the gift of God and who it is that asks you for a drink, you would have asked him and he would have given you living water."
>
> "Sir," the woman said, "you have nothing to draw with and the well is deep. Where can you get this living water? Are you greater than our father Jacob, who gave us the well and drank from it himself, as did also his sons and his flocks and herds?"
>
> Jesus answered, "Everyone who drinks this water will be thirsty again, but whoever drinks the water I give him will never thirst. Indeed, the water I give him will become in him a spring of water welling up to eternal life."
>
> The woman said to him, "Sir, give me this water so that I won't get thirsty and have to keep coming here to draw water." (John 4:10–15)

Jesus never used insider jargon. He was enigmatic, almost mysterious, using metaphor and poetic language to intrigue. He mentioned the name of God, but avoided theological terms. He certainly didn't mention the resurrection or the correct site of Yahweh worship, two issues that divided Jews and Samaritans. Instead, he painted a picture of the gift he would give, with words designed to evoke a strong yearning in that arid, lifeless setting—drink, water, thirst, spring, welling, living.

When I first became a follower of Jesus, the language spoken in church often stumped me. "Are you born again?" Christians would ask. *What?* I'd think, as confused as Nicodemus (John

3:3–5) but too hesitant to ask for clarification. "We're washed in the blood of the lamb," the choir sang. I shuddered, picturing brutal animal sacrifices in Hindu temples. "You'll find more orders of worship in the narthex," the usher told me when I arrived late. I had no idea he was talking about the pieces of paper everybody else was holding. *More evangelicalese*, I'd mutter when I finally caught on, stocking the phrase away for future reference.

Our diplomats-in-training can't overhear us speaking "evangelicalese" with people outside or even inside the church. As we describe our spiritual life, they must hear us choose words with creativity and imagination. We hope our kids, who learn languages ten times faster than we do, will surpass our abilities to invoke intrigue about God through conversation.

## Jesus Knew the Woman's True Self

Early in their calling, ambassador children must learn a significant truth about the human condition: everybody longs to be known. We all want to be identified not by mistakes and messes, nor by a list of successes and accomplishments, but recognized as our true selves—the people we were designed to be. The poet Matthew Arnold expressed this desire in "The Buried Life":

> But often, in the world's most crowded streets,
> But often, in the din of strife,
> There rises an unspeakable desire
> After the knowledge of our buried life;
> A thirst to spend our fire and restless force
> In tracking out our true, original course;
> A longing to inquire
> Into the mystery of this heart that beats
> So wild, so deep in us—to know
> Whence our lives come, and where they go.[3]

85

The third kingdom purpose of human interaction, then, is to *know*. The Samaritan woman at the well and Jesus both were familiar with the story of Hagar, Sarah's maidservant who bore Abraham's oldest son, Ishmael. Once Isaac was born, Sarah and Abraham banished Hagar into the desert, where God met her beside a well. Michael Card tells Hagar's story well:

> She wanders out into the desert on the road to Shur. But she is not really alone, even as we can never really be. The angel of the Lord meets her near an as yet nameless spring and asks, "Where have you come from and where are you going?" It is a basic question we should still be constantly asking ourselves. She honestly opens her heart to the angel. "I'm running away," she defiantly whispers through her tears.
>
> The angel tells the frightened girl to do the last thing in the world she wants to do, return to the abuse from which she has fled. In the language of poetry, he promises her that there is more going on than she can see, more than she can possibly know. It is a heartbreakingly beautiful picture, the angel singing a song of hope in the desert to a hopeless pregnant girl.
>
> As the angel finishes his song (vs. 11–12), Hagar abruptly responds to the angel who knew her name. She speaks to God a new name, Lahai Roi, "The One who sees me." In her fear, hopelessness and despair, God met her in the wilderness with His perfect provision. It was all she really needed or wanted. She wanted simply to be seen, and the God who sees, saw her and sang to her a song of hope.[4]

The parallel between God's encounter with Hagar and Jesus' encounter with this rejected Samaritan woman is uncanny. God saw them both beside a well and knew them both. But the Samaritan woman, like most of us, tried to avoid those seeing eyes. She retreated from intimacy, even with Jesus essentially pleading: *If only you knew me! How I want you to know me!*

"Sir," she said, "you have nothing to draw with and the well is deep. Where can you get this living water? Are you greater than our father Jacob, who gave us the well and drank from it himself, as did also his sons and his flocks and herds?"

In a desert culture, access to water is a source of power. When this woman reminded Jesus of his inability to draw water, she was trying to recover the position of power in their encounter. *She* was the one with the water jar; *he* was the one who was thirsty. Why was *he* talking about giving *her* water? Just who did he think he was? I can imagine the sarcasm in her tone: "Are you greater than Jacob?"

Anybody else would have given up the pursuit of intimacy at this point. But Jesus went on to discuss the very issues she raised—control, power, and access to water. "Everyone who drinks *this* water will be thirsty again, but whoever drinks the water I give . . . will never thirst. Indeed, the water I give . . . will become in that person a spring of water welling up to eternal life." He affirmed her secret longing to be a powerful giver of water. He knew she was designed to be a source of water, of love, of life; she was supposed to quench other people's thirst.

"Sir," she said, "give me this water so that I won't get thirsty and have to keep coming here to draw water."

Jesus must have heard some weariness in her voice; a hint of her self-imposed loneliness. He cut to the heart of her problem with intimacy. "Go, call your husband and come back."

"I have no husband," she replied.

Then Jesus went on to show her exactly how well he knew her: "You are right when you say you have no husband. The fact is, you have had five husbands, and the man you now have is not your husband. What you have just said is quite true" (freely quoted from John 4:11–18).

The Samaritan woman must have been astounded. This man had known about her history of broken relationships *before* asking her for water. Fully aware of her shame and sin, he had offered her access to power, water, even a mysterious gift of God.

Unlike Jesus, we don't have a divine view into people's souls. But as ambassador families, we can practice the skill of discernment. We can develop the art of listening and reading faces, gleaning insight into the interior lives and suffering of people we encounter. In our conversations with and about others, we can unveil for our kids the universal human longing for intimacy.

When our boys commented on the scanty clothing worn by some pop icons, for example, we discussed how such in-your-face sexuality is often a cry for attention not received during childhood. "If she'd felt beloved and valued as a girl," I explained, "she wouldn't have such an extreme longing to be desired and noticed by others as a young woman." Hopefully, our sons got the message that condemnation is not on the list of Christian responsibilities, while mercy and compassion are top priorities.

## Jesus Revealed His True Self

The fourth purpose of diplomatic communication is to *reveal* truth about our homeland—including the identity of our King.

Once confronted with how well Jesus knew her, the woman again took a step back and tried to hide behind theological dispute. "Sir," she said quickly, "I can see that you are a prophet. Our fathers worshiped on this mountain, but you Jews claim that the place where we must worship is in Jerusalem."

Jesus answered, "Believe me, woman, a time is coming when you will worship the Father neither on this mountain nor in Jerusalem. You Samaritans worship what you do not know; we worship what we do know, for salvation is from the Jews. Yet a time is coming and has now come when the true worshipers will worship the Father in spirit and truth, for they are the kind of worshipers the Father seeks. God is spirit, and his worshipers must worship in spirit and in truth."

Once again, he affirmed this lonely, suffering woman. He described her as a true worshiper. He told her that God was seeking her; wanted to know her; would draw near to her.

The woman answered, "I know that Messiah is coming. When he comes, he will explain everything to us."

Jesus then made an amazing declaration of his identity: "I who speak to you am he" (freely quoted from John 4:19–26). This was the boldest statement he had made to date about his identity. In fact, just before this encounter, we learn that he did not "entrust himself" to some who believed, "for he knew all [people]" (John 2:23–24). Instead, he chose to reveal his identity to a loner, a foreign woman, a shady character. What a step of trust!

This was also a classic example of the diplomatic lifestyle as observed by his "children"—the disciples. They ignored this woman when they finally entered the scene, but witnessed a powerful transformation during the next two days. By the time Jesus left Samaria, the woman at the well had become a leader and the giver of the water of life to many. Her entire village knew the identity of the man who had connected with her by asking for help, intrigued her with his language, and recognized her true self.

On a children's fiction discussion e-list where I lurk but seldom make the effort to communicate, I'm impressed by one or two followers of Jesus who leap into the most fiery of discussions. Using winsome, humorous writing, they shatter stereotypes of book-burning zealots who can't appreciate literature that's not "approved by card-carrying Christians."

On the Net, and in other realms of pop culture, modern-day versions of the Samaritan woman are waiting for savvy and sincere followers of Jesus to meet *them* in the desert. As ambassador families, we venture there expectantly, using the vernacular to connect, intrigue, know others, and reveal truth.

## Focus Story: The Net

Dwayne was tired of seeing the back of his daughter's head silhouetted against the glow of the computer screen. "You've been online for hours, Amber. Don't you have homework?"

"I finished it," Amber answered.

"What have you been doing for so long?"

"Six of my friends are online. We're having a big free-for-all about God. It's awesome."

"That's great, honey, but wouldn't it be better to talk about that kind of stuff face-to-face?" Dwayne thought about the nuances of nonverbal communication that helped so much when talking with his friends about God—the gleam of interest in someone's eye, the furrowed brow, the averted gaze, the long pause.

"IM-ing is awesome, Dad. You can come in and out of the conversation if you want. You can listen in if you want and not say anything. Besides, six people can chat at a time, so it builds community."

Dwayne leaned over his daughter's shoulder. "what do u think rose," Amy was typing.

"You get A's in English, Amber," he muttered. "No question marks, no caps, misspellings . . ."

"Dad, chill out and listen to what Rose has to say."

". . . how could he luv me. . . . duz he see the cuts under my sleeves. . . . duz he hear me crying in my room at night. . . ."

Dwayne waited breathlessly to see how Amber would answer.

"Uhh, Dad? Do you mind? I can't think with you breathing down my neck."

"Oh. Okay. I'll just head back to my recliner then."

Dwayne sank back into his chair, frowning. Amber spent hours chatting with her friends online. Good conversations might be taking place in cyberspace, but you couldn't hold someone's hand through a screen. *And that's what Rose needs,*

Dwayne thought. *A smiley-face emoticon can't comfort like a friend's hand holding yours.*

## Put It into Practice

1. Francis de Laboulaye, French Ambassador to Brazil, Japan, and the United States, said, "One simple definition of diplomacy is that it is the oral aspect of international relations. There is an essential difference between what is written and what is spoken, not only because spoken words are essentially more ephemeral (*verba volant*), but because the spoken language has infinitely more nuances, being both richer and more subtle than written texts."[5] Do you agree with de Laboulaye? Why or why not?

2. To what extent can we connect, intrigue, know, and reveal truth through technologies like computers and cell phones? How do these technologies compare with each other and with face-to-face interactions? What do we lose? What do we gain?

3. Do any of these four purposes of communication as demonstrated by Jesus' interaction with the Samaritan woman come easily to you (connect, intrigue, know, reveal)? Which one is most difficult? Why?

4. Read the last three stanzas of Matthew Arnold's "The Buried Life." Be mindful of any lines or phrases that seem especially significant.

> But often, in the world's most crowded streets,
> But often, in the din of strife,
> There rises an unspeakable desire
> After the knowledge of our buried life;
> A thirst to spend our fire and restless force
> In tracking out our true, original course;

A longing to inquire
Into the mystery of this heart that beats
So wild, so deep in us—to know
Whence our lives come, and where they go.
And many a man in his own breast then delves,
But deep enough, alas, none ever mines.
And we have been on many thousand lines,
And we have shown, on each, spirit and power;
But hardly have we, for one little hour,
Been on our own line, have we been ourselves—
Hardly had skill to utter one of all
The nameless feelings that course through our breast,
But they course on for ever unexpressed,
And long we try in vain to speak and act
Our hidden self, and what we say and do
Is eloquent, is well—but 'tis not true!
And then we will no more be racked
With inward striving, and demand
Of all the thousand nothings of the hour
Their stupefying power;
Ah yes, and they benumb us at our call!
Yet still, from time to time, vague and forlorn,
From the soul's subterranean depth upborne
As from an infinitely distant land,
Come airs, and floating echoes, and convey
A melancholy into all our day.

Only—but this is rare—
When a beloved hand is laid in ours,
When, jaded with the rush and glare
Of the interminable hours,
Our eyes can in another's eyes read clear,
When our world-deafened ear
Is by the tones of a loved voice caressed—
A bolt is shot back somewhere in our breast,
And a lost pulse of feeling stirs again.
The eye sinks inward, and the heart lies plain,

And what we mean, we say, and what we would, we
    know.
A man becomes aware of his life's flow,
And hears its winding murmur; and he sees
The meadows where it glides, the sun, the breeze.

And there arrives a lull in the hot race
Wherein he doth for ever chase
That flying and elusive shadow, rest.
An air of coolness plays upon his face,
And an unwonted calm pervades his breast.
And then he thinks he knows
The hills where his life rose,
And the sea where it goes.


## Bringing It Home (for the Family or Small Group)

5. Name a slang phrase that is (or was) frequently spoken by your generation to encourage or affirm. Name another that is (or was) used to insult or demean. Discuss the origins of the phrases.

6. Employ your dramatic skills and stage the following scene. Parent(s), pretend you're a teenager working as a clerk at the grocery store. Kid(s), you're a middle-aged shopper. Using the vernacular of the generation that is not yours, discuss a mistake in the price of your groceries. Evaluate your success and failure in communicating after the scene is over.

7. Tell the others in the group how somebody on the opposite end of the social or spiritual spectrum helped you recently. What did you feel toward the person after the interaction? How do you think they felt about you?

8. Plan something intriguing to say about God or your faith this week to a person who has never talked about spiritual things with you. Or simply mention Jesus' name

as though he were a friend or family member you see every day. Watch the other person's reaction. Does her body language change (i.e., did she take a step back, fold her arms, look away)? Be ready to tell others in this group about the interaction.

9. Does your family have rules or limits that govern communication via technology (i.e., time spent on computers or phones)? Do you think these rules are fair? Given: Spending MORE time techno-communicating would foster connection, intimacy, interest in God, and the revelation of truth. Split your small group in half randomly to prepare the two sides of the debate, or parents take the "pro" position, and kids argue the "con" position.

# 6

# Following Jesus When
# Others Judge You

Diplomacy is the art of letting someone have your way.

Daniele Vare[1]

During my undergraduate years at college, I felt that many
white Americans registered that the fact that I was "Asian"
before noticing I was a woman. I was looking forward to
spending a year in India during graduate school. Finally, I
could fit in as "one of us," and be perceived as a woman first.
I donned *salwar kameez* outfits and sarees and joyfully began
my experiment.

It didn't work. From the beginning, I stuck out like a bride's
hand without henna. An American diet had made me taller
and stronger-looking than most Indian women, and I talked
and walked differently than they did. To my delight, though,

strangers kept asking if I were an Indian television star—a couple of them even wanted my autograph. I set them straight, flung my hair back, and donned dark glasses as I sauntered off. *Finally*, I thought, *I stand out from the crowd for the RIGHT reasons.*

Halfway through the year, a cousin gently suggested I watch the show featuring the actress I was supposed to resemble. I watched in disgust as my immensely unattractive look-alike made a fool of herself, accompanied by much canned laughter. Enduring the attention as good-naturedly as possible during the rest of my time in India, I slipped back into my American minority "invisibility cloak" with a sigh of relief.

Looking like a native in India that year was a liability. While traveling in other countries, though, having dark hair, skin, and eyes has usually been a boon—I look somewhat like the citizens of more than half the countries of the world. It's easier to blend in, avoid tourist prices, and be treated like an insider. But when I look like the people on the margin of a culture, traveling becomes tough.

When my appearance associated me with an oppressed or despised minority group, I've caught myself trying to correct mistaken impressions. In California, for example, I wielded my American accent and college-educated vocabulary so that others could distinguish me from illegal Hispanic immigrants. In Paris, I dressed even more modestly than I usually do, aware that I resembled the Brazilian prostitutes who solicited customers along the Seine. In Thailand, my American accent set me apart from the generally disliked group of Indian business owners. After the terrorist attacks of 9/11, I found myself making small talk with airport security guards so they could hear my voice and realize that I wasn't from the Middle East. As I became conscious of my efforts to align myself with the powerful, I remembered uneasily how Jesus went out of his way to associate with the powerless.

96

## You're "One of Them"

It's natural to want to avoid affiliation with a subculture that's despised. Many of our peers, both inside and outside the church, judge the pop culture of our kids' generation as completely depraved or worthless. Educated highbrows look down at current trends, classifying them as "low" culture. Not only is our ambassador lifestyle condemned by middle-aged intellectuals—many in the church believe that true followers of Jesus shouldn't become too familiar with popular culture. The integrity of our faith comes into question if we're up to speed about "what's hot." How can we listen to *that* music? How can we let our kids read *that* book? *Those movies are inappropriate for Christians to watch.* They wonder, *Are those people really believers?*

Christians who judge the ambassador family typically don't listen to anything but "Christian" music or read books sold in Christian Bookseller's Association bookstores. They try to keep their kids safe by encouraging friendships with kids raised by like-minded parents. The people of God should live counterculturally, they argue, recognized by the distinct holiness of our lives. The lost will see the truth of the gospel only as we "shine like stars in a crooked and depraved generation" (adapted from Philippians 2:15).

I respect the zeal for holiness in this kind of countercultural parenting. In an age of compromise and laziness, where prosperity and self-indulgence have diluted the church until we're flavorless and unable to "salt" society, these parents are serious about raising disciples of a cross-bearing Man. They are aware of how culture wants to control us and are making an effort to resist that pressure. The problem arises when their zeal for holiness leads them to an error in judgment about *our* mission. They think we lead our kids into pop culture solely for enjoyment or entertainment. But we want our kids to do more than just resist the pressure of culture; we're trying to train visionaries

97

who can affect culture for the sake of our home country. While having some fun is inevitable, our modus operandi is to train ambassadors of Jesus Christ to transform the host country.

### You're Too Intense

Another type of Christian altogether might judge us for being too serious—*What's wrong with the wholehearted pursuit of fun?* they ask. I respect the freedom in Christ such people promote. To a world that views the church as a dull, confined place, they demonstrate the joy and abundant life we inherit as children of God. They are aware of the potential in culture's offerings, and open to discovering God's presence there.

The problem arises when this so-called "quest for freedom" is actually laziness in disguise. Some people want the freedom of forgiveness without attempting the narrow, uphill climb of discipleship—which manifests itself in the vocation of parenting as strenuous effort and prayer.

"We don't let our kids play video games," a woman once informed me. "They're way too violent."

"Oh, we let ours play all they want," said another. "What's the big deal?"

The first woman turned to me. As a pastor's wife, I'm sometimes considered an expert on a variety of subjects. (Little do they know.) "Does your family own a gaming console?" she asked.

I frowned. I was reluctant to justify the existence of our console. I didn't want to detail the limitations we imposed on our preteens about time and ratings, or explain that I read reams of reviews before sanctioning the purchase of a new game. Did I have to defend ourselves by describing how my husband and I often sat on the couch and watched them game (with Rob sometimes responding to the boys' insistent invitations by playing along)? Feebly and a bit resentfully, I outlined the way we were trying to travel with our boys into the realm of gaming before they became teenagers.

Both women looked doubtful. "Isn't it easier just to get rid of the console? How can you be sure they won't get hooked on violence and adrenaline?" the first woman asked.

"You can't be sure," I had to admit. "But we're trying to prepare them to make wise choices when they're at a friend's house, or on their own in the future. Also, to discern the human need for quest and challenge which the games satisfy."

The second woman shook her head. "To tell you the truth, that sounds kind of controlling. And exhausting. I don't have time to do all that research. I've got to just trust my kids on this one."

I sighed. The effort we spent on learning about gaming wasn't about control and suspicion. It was about journeying together as long as our kids still wanted our company, seeking truth and beauty, recognizing evil and degradation, learning about ourselves, and understanding the intrigue of gaming to other preteens and teenagers. But how could I explain that to these women?

When other Christians don't understand our methods of parenting, they secretly (or publicly) label us either as idolaters or control freaks. "You're conforming to the world's standards," one group concludes. Others disagree: "Take it easy! You're too intense about parenting." It's hard to be judged by your own people. But we can take heart from the Gospels. While our King walked the planet, he aligned himself so much with Samaritans that he was actually accused of being "one of them": "Aren't we right in saying that you are a Samaritan and demon-possessed?" they asked him (John 8:48).

Perhaps aware that Samaritans were or would be listening to his words, Jesus didn't refute the accusation of being a Samaritan. He let that label stand. He did, however, go on to argue that he wasn't demon-possessed.

And there's no question that Jesus was exhausted by the time and effort he spent training his "children." He needed more than one break for solitude, a heartening sign for those of us who are parents. John wrote that "Jesus did many other miraculous signs in the presence of his disciples, which are not recorded in this book" (John 20:30). Why perform miracles for the eyes of a few unless you were deliberately trying to prepare them for a future of service? This nurture of a small group of people was the primary focus of Jesus' life; he was the one who set a high standard for purposeful parenting. Child rearing requires a substantial investment of time, thought, and energy, especially if we're ambassadors of the King.

## Changing Our Travel Plans

Are we called to curtail our ventures into pop culture when other Christians object? In Richard Curtis's lighthearted flick, *Love Actually*, one of my favorite subplots involves two actors who portray "body doubles" in the filming of sexually graphic scenes. Even as the pair undress and grope one another for the sake of the movie within the movie, they embark on a shy and sweet courtship that is almost old-fashioned in its progress. Slyly, Richard Curtis underlines how intimacy between a man and a woman is so much more than naked skin against naked skin.

While I enjoyed the satire of this subplot, I might forgo any scenes that included nudity if I were watching with someone who battled the snare of pornography. Would the irony I enjoyed be worth the temptation my friend might endure? I'd also probably not suggest the movie as appropriate fare for a teenager. Could a younger viewer understand the nuances of Curtis's humor, or would she interpret my endorsement as license to watch other, more exploitative graphic films?

I'm wary of endorsing or recommending products of pop culture in general. Because I write books for young readers, many Christian parents asked if I thought their kids should read the Harry Potter books. This was always a tough one to answer, because I knew the intent of their question. They wanted to know what I thought about a series of books featuring witches and wizards as good guys.

"Did you let your kids read them?" they asked. That was an easier question to answer. I was mortified by the myopic Harry Potter–bashing in the church, given our easygoing acceptance of characters like Glinda in the *Wizard of Oz* and Gandalf in the *Lord of the Rings*. Rob and I did teach the boys how the Bible views witchcraft (recounting the story of the witch of Endor and Saul in 1 Samuel 28). If we'd glimpsed even the slightest attraction to the occult in our boys' lives, our discussion about Harry Potter might have focused more on the dangers of dabbling in it. But the bottom line was that for our family, the Harry Potter books were a jolly good read, a first-class ticket to a world of imagination and adventure.

That's why I wanted to answer with a resounding "yes" when acquaintances asked if *their* kids should read J. K. Rowling's work. But I didn't. What if one of those young people slipped beyond Harry Potter into spin-off books that outline the practice of spells, incantations, or the Wicca religion? I didn't know most of the kids who might be affected by my endorsement. Instead of giving the easy answer my friends wanted, I asked *them* questions like: "What else are your kids reading on their own? What are you reading together as a family? How does this reading affect the relationships between your kids, you, their friends who aren't followers of Jesus, and God?" We should be asking these types of questions of every book we consider reading, I thought, not just Harry Potter. But part of me felt I'd copped out. Why couldn't I just respond: "Yes, read the books, they're a lot of fun!" That's what I really believed.

101

My hesitation to endorse or recommend was related to the issue Paul addresses in his first letter to the Corinthians:

> Be careful, however, that the exercise of your freedom does not become a stumbling block to the weak. For if anyone with a weak conscience sees you who have this knowledge eating in an idol's temple, won't he be emboldened to eat what has been sacrificed to idols? So this weak brother, for whom Christ died, is destroyed by your knowledge. When you sin against your brothers in this way and wound their weak conscience, you sin against Christ. Therefore, if what I eat causes my brother to fall into sin, I will never eat meat again, so that I will not cause him to fall. (1 Cor. 8:9–13)

We limit our forays into pop culture only if it might damage a brother or sister in Christ. Our behavior might be raising painful memories from the past or bringing temptation into the present—only God understands the human heart. Our call is to emulate our King by responding with mercy instead of arrogance to those who judge us. We don't join in the outcry of people who condemn some Christians as narrow-minded; we respond to legalism in the lives of our brothers and sisters with love and grace.

But must we give up *all* diplomatic trips into pop culture for the sake of other Christians? Paul went on to discuss this later in his letter:

> "Everything is permissible"—but not everything is beneficial. "Everything is permissible"—but not everything is constructive. Nobody should seek his own good, but the good of others.
>
> Eat anything sold in the meat market without raising questions of conscience, for, "The earth is the Lord's, and everything in it."
>
> If some unbeliever invites you to a meal and you want to go, eat whatever is put before you without raising questions of conscience. But if anyone says to you, "This has been of-

fered in sacrifice," then do not eat it, both for the sake of the man who told you and for conscience' sake—the other man's conscience, I mean, not yours. For why should my freedom be judged by another's conscience? If I take part in the meal with thankfulness, why am I denounced because of something I thank God for?

So whether you eat or drink or whatever you do, do it all for the glory of God. Do not cause anyone to stumble, whether Jews, Greeks or the church of God. (1 Cor. 10:23–32)

What was Paul's advice? Partake freely of anything sold in the market or offered by unbelievers—the whole earth belongs to God! What a hearty affirmation of the ambassador lifestyle! But he offered one qualification—the only time to limit ourselves in seeking God's presence far and wide is out of love for another person. If I'm consuming something that bothers the conscience of another person journeying with me, it's my duty to stop. Either I wait for my companion to receive freedom so that we might travel together, or I venture into that particular realm without that person around. While I don't internalize his or her legalism (i.e., let my freedom be judged by their conscience), I take Paul's advice "not to eat" in that particular instance for my friend's sake. Once we get home, I explain to my kids why we turned off the movie or the music or changed the subject of conversation. It was for the sake of the other person's conscience—not because God was displeased with what we were doing or saying.

Sometimes this difference of opinion between Christians takes place under the same roof. It's tough to live in a home where parents have different ideas of what constitutes sin, but not impossible with God's grace. Mom's watching a reality show, for example, that Dad thinks is unedifying. They discuss their points of view; Dad states his reservations, Mom explains why she wants to watch the show. Christian maturity limits them to two possible scenarios. In the first, Dad leaves the room

103

and lets Mom watch on her own without making shaming or judgmental remarks. Alternatively, if Dad believes strongly that "consuming" the show would be compromising the family's integrity, Mom turns it off without insisting on her freedom. Their kids realize that while she isn't convinced that it would be sinful to watch the show, she values her relationship with Dad more than her own self-indulgence. Ideally, truthful conversation, respect, and prayer characterize the whole interaction.

At the movie theater, this hypothetical couple's daughter might be the one to suggest, "Let's go bowling, guys," when she notes the discomfort of a friend. As the whole family modifies their sojourns into pop culture for the sake of other people, the kids learn to practice God's priority of love. Ambassador families travel boldly, but take a different turn here or there, or stop for a while to let companions catch up.

The only time Paul insists on exercising freedom is to remove a barrier from the path of people who do not yet follow Christ:

> When Peter came to Antioch, I opposed him to his face, because he was in the wrong. Before certain men came from James, he used to eat with the Gentiles. But when they arrived, he began to draw back and separate himself from the Gentiles because he was afraid of those who belonged to the circumcision group. (Gal. 2:11–12)

Paul calls us to defend valiantly the incredible freedom of the gospel. In the scenarios above, for example, Mom would explain in the presence of the kids why she thinks watching that show wouldn't displease God, and yet she turns it off for Dad's sake. In turn, if another Christian forcefully promotes legalism, their daughter speaks up: "I don't think watching this movie would be a sin, but let's do something else if a few of us are bothered by it." Such responses reveal to a watching world that Christianity is not about a set of rules, and that we value love more than anything.

In the book of Revelation, as in other parts of the Bible, the metaphor of white clothing is used several times: "Yet you have a few people in Sardis who have not soiled their clothes. They will walk with me, dressed in white, for they are worthy" (Rev. 3:4). I used to think that pristine white clothes represented a life untarnished by the world—until I visited Calcutta. There, Mother Teresa and her Sisters of Charity were clothed in white. Instead of staying cloistered away from a world of need, they wandered the muddy streets, caring for the destitute and dying people who clutched at the hems of their white sarees. What a metaphor for our call to be ambassadors! We receive the royal white robes of our King's purity when we become citizens of the kingdom, but daily we comb the streets and alleys of culture for the sake of the dying and destitute.

In forming our response to religious people who condemn us as "Samaritans" or even "demon-possessed," we refer again and always to Jesus. He spoke the truth in freedom, and yet set out resolutely to offer his life for religious people, Samaritans, *and* the demon-possessed—the ultimate self-denial for the sake of others.

### Focus Story: Style

The woman beside them in the pew was paying more attention to Jan and Jenny than to the sermon. As they stood up to sing the closing hymn, Jan sensed the disapproving glare fixed on Jenny's short skirt and tight, sleeveless T-shirt. *I should have made Jenny wear the dress her grandmother sent,* Jan thought. Then she glanced at her daughter, who was using her beautiful alto voice to sing the harmony line of "Joyful, Joyful, We Adore Thee." *Why should I let an old grump decide which battles to fight with my daughter?* Jan asked herself. *It is for freedom that Christ has set us free!*

105

They stopped by the grocery store on the way home. Jan noticed several middle-aged men leering at Jenny's legs and curves. *I should have made her wear the dress her grandmother sent,* she thought again. She watched Jenny play peek-a-boo with a wailing baby, applying expert babysitting skills to elicit smiles from the child and his harried mother. *Why should I let a few dirty old men decide how my daughter should dress?* Jan asked herself. *It is for freedom that Christ has set us free!*

At the checkout counter, Jenny leaned forward confidentially. "Mom, check out the tattoo on that girl's ankle," she whispered. "I'm getting mine on the top of my foot. Don't you think that's a better place?"

*What? A TATTOO? No way! Time to head into battle,* Jan thought, taking a deep breath. *Freedom in Christ doesn't mean that a trendy fifteen-year-old can scar her skin for life.* "We'll talk about it when we get home, Jenny," she said.

## Put It into Practice

1. Have you ever felt judged by others about your interactions with popular culture? How did you respond?

2. Has another person's free enjoyment of any aspect of pop culture ever led you into temptation or caused you to sin?

3. Is there a proper way for Christians to dress, or is it permissible for us to clothe ourselves like our peers? When, if ever, should we restrict our freedom in style? When you have time for Bible study, reflect on the following Bible verses, asking God how you should dress: Deuteronomy 22:5; Matthew 6:25; 1 Corinthians 6:19–20; Colossians 3:12; 1 Timothy 2:9; James 2:1–4; and 1 Peter 3:3.

4. Read the following excerpt of an article:

"Christian items are such a hot trend right now," said Jaye Hersh, owner of a boutique that sells some of the Jesus chic items. "Madonna has been wearing 'Jesus Is My Homeboy,' so that kind of started the trend because she is such a *fashionista* and whatever she wears goes. Then it's kind of trickled down to other celebrities."

Jesus wear has long been available in Christian apparel stores, but now it's popping up in mainstream chains like Urban Outfitters.

"It's everywhere. It's at all the stores," said Craig Gross, founder of XXXchurch.com. "This is the latest thing. A lot of people are wearing them not because they want to display their relationship with God, but because it's the cool thing to do."

Inevitably, some are insulted by the Ts and accessories bearing Christ's name and image. "A lot of people find it offensive and say you can't put Jesus on a shirt," Gross said.

One of those people is Los Angeles attorney Michael Allan, who grew up Catholic. "I think these T-shirts are disrespectful," Allan said. "Mary and Jesus don't belong on T-shirts. There are other ways to show your devotion."[2]

Do you think Christians should display verses or religious slogans on clothes, cars, and other paraphernalia? Why or why not?

5. During the nineteenth century, despite the condemnation and disapproval of his Western colleagues, missionary Hudson Taylor wore his hair in a pigtail, used chopsticks, and donned Chinese robes to preach the gospel to the Chinese people. For ambassador purposes, is it ever appropriate to dress like the natives of popular culture?

## Bringing It Home (for the Family or Small Group)

6. Some Christians set a standard for the way girls should dress:

   > God's purpose for a woman sexually is to "intoxicate" *one man* with her sensual beauty. A woman or young girl is absolutely worthy of the stares that may come her way, but God says that the unique characteristics of her sensual beauty are to be treasured secrets—secrets to keep for one man. When a girl dresses immodestly, she creates arousal in many men. That is missing the purpose of God's carefully crafted masterpiece. Is it just fashion? No. Immodesty is sin. And we must call it that.[3]

   In strict Muslim societies, a woman is required to cover herself from head to toe to keep a man from sinning. Is the onus on a woman to dress modestly, the responsibility of men to battle lust, or is some combination of two required by God?

7. Five hundred kids attended a Junior High Bash at All Saints Parish in Manassas, Virginia. The *Arlington Catholic Herald* reported that "After attending Mass, members of the Arlington Catholic Youth Board performed a 'Modesty Fashion Show,' which was met with an enthusiastic response by the younger teens. The show featured appropriate outfits for a variety of settings such as church, school, and outdoors, sprinkled with suggestions on how to dress in a trendy, yet modest, way."[4] Kids: Is it possible to be trendy and modest at the same time? What would such an outfit look like? Head for your parents' closets and pull together some "trendy yet modest" outfits for your parents to wear in a family or small group style show. Alternatively, flip through magazines and find outfits that might have been featured in the Manassas fashion show.

8. Parents, if you could change one thing about your child's outward adornment, what would it be and why? Kids, how do you feel about your parents' suggestion? Kids, if you could change one thing about your parents' outward adornment, what would it be and why? Parents, how do you feel about your kids' suggestion?

# Diplomatic Essentials

# 7

## Patriotism

A diplomat is nothing but a headwaiter who is allowed to sit down occasionally.

Peter Ustinov[1]

Each year about 25,000 people register to take the U.S. Foreign Service exam, but the State Department hires only about 400 of them. The exam serves as the first elimination tool. How are you tested? Mostly, you have to know a lot about the United States of America. Among other things, you answer questions about the country's history, culture, economics, education and politics, the Constitution, and the structure of the government. The bottom line is that you have to know your country well in order to represent it.

It also helps to love your country. A good friend has served the U.S. State Department for over a decade. In an e-mail, he defined a challenge faced by some foreign service officers:

"It's critical to always keep at the front of your mind your primary purpose, to represent the interests of your country. To do otherwise risks being labeled as having 'gone native' and reducing your effectiveness as a diplomat and a representative of your nation."[2]

As a first-generation immigrant, I can understand the tension of identifying with two countries. My citizenship is American. I'm so grateful for the opportunities and freedom I enjoy in this country and I pledge complete allegiance to the Stars and Stripes. But at the same time, it's hard to place my hand over my heart because I cherish the Bengali heritage that dwells there. I decided not to attempt the U.S. Foreign Service Exam because of this cultural schizophrenia, even though many political science majors took it as a matter of course. I wasn't sure I could unflinchingly support U.S. interests if I were posted to India.[3]

## Dual Citizenship for Diplomats?

In 1849, the prominent American diplomat George Bancroft observed that "A country should as soon tolerate a man with two wives as a man with two countries, as soon bear with polygamy as that state of double allegiance which common sense so repudiates that it has not even coined a word to express it."[4]

Others disagree. Over ninety countries recognize dual citizenship. In 2001, of about 1.5 million legal immigrants to the United States, 90 percent came from countries that allow some form of dual citizenship. Dr. Stanley A. Rensho of the City University of New York sees this as a disaster for America:

> Should we allow Americans to serve in the foreign government of other countries? My answer is no. Should we allow

them to serve in some capacity in the armed forces of other governments? My answer is no. Should they be allowed to vote in other countries? My answer is unequivocally no. No country, and especially no democracy, can afford to have large numbers of citizens with shallow civic and national attachments.[5]

While the question of permitting dual nationalities for regular citizens is up for debate, U.S. Foreign Service officers are usually not allowed the privilege:

When an individual acts in such a way as to indicate a preference for a foreign country over the United States ... he or she may be prone to provide information or make decisions that are harmful to the interests of the United States. Conditions that could raise a security concern and may be disqualifying include the exercise of dual citizenship.[6]

Even the American ideal of free speech is qualified for diplomats: "As public servants, Foreign Service Officers must publicly defend U.S. government policy, despite personal reservations."[7]

Historically, the best diplomats are single-minded patriots who identify strongly with the country of their citizenship. As ambassadors representing Jesus, then, we can't be dual citizens with equally strong ties to both host and home countries. Our primary allegiance is to an unseen realm where our King reigns over his subjects.

To serve effectively as ambassadors in popular culture, our children must be wholeheartedly devoted to the kingdom of heaven with a passion akin to patriotism. We prepare them for their diplomatic post by teaching them the lore and law of our homeland, fostering ties to the community, and cultivating a deep love of the King.

## Teaching the Lore and Law of the Land

When kids with a Judeo-Christian heritage from the neighborhood visit, I seize the opportunity to take an informal survey.

"Hey, Matt. Ever heard of David and Goliath?"

"Ummm . . . nope."

"Know any of the Ten Commandments?"

"Ummmm . . . nope."

"Okay. Last question. What's Easter all about?"

"Oh, the Easter bunny and spring and stuff."

The level of biblical illiteracy in America is staggering. Huge numbers of Americans confess to be Christians, and yet know next to nothing about what's actually in the Bible. This ignorance can't be characteristic of ambassadors—we need enough biblical knowledge and theological understanding to pass an imaginary heavenly version of the foreign service exam. The responsibility to teach our kids about the Bible falls on our shoulders. We can't rely on fifty or so Sunday School classes each year to explain theology, or on occasional Hollywood blockbusters and animated vegetables to teach the stories of the Bible.

Bible study with our kids requires time, thought, and preparation. In the eighteenth century, Susana Wesley was the paragon who raised Charles (hymn-writer par excellence) and John (founder of Methodism) along with at least eight other children. She appointed one hour a week to teach each child about God and answer his or her spiritual questions. Our calendar, too, should include a regular chunk of time set apart to read and study the Bible with our kids. But passing on familiarity with biblical stories and lessons also happens spontaneously, in the goings out and comings in of daily life. Moses left detailed instructions about this continual process:

Hear, O Israel: The LORD our God, the LORD is one. Love the LORD your God with all your heart and with all your soul

116

and with all your strength. These commandments that I give you today are to be upon your hearts. Impress them on your children. Talk about them when you sit at home and when you walk along the road, when you lie down and when you get up. Tie them as symbols on your hands and bind them on your foreheads. Write them on the doorframes of your houses and on your gates. (Deut. 6:4–9)

"Impressing" children with biblical truth sometimes works best if you can help them apply truths in tough times. When a crotchety teacher's aide misunderstood and wrongly punished one of our children, for example, we tried to listen sympathetically to our son's frustration and disappointment. Later, at bedtime, we read the story of Daniel together and encouraged our son to emulate Daniel by trusting God to come to his defense. The Scripture helped our son face his own "lion" at school the next day, and his application of it made Daniel's experience come alive for all of us.

While it's crucial for parents to read through the Bible ourselves from cover to cover, I wouldn't recommend forcing kids to read from page one of Genesis through the end of Revelation. My own introduction to the Bible came during my freshman year of college, when a humanities professor assigned the book of Genesis as required reading. Grumbling and short of money, I purchased the whole Bible as one of our required texts. I read through the first few chapters of Genesis, but couldn't understand a word. What did this ancient, poetical story about fruit, trees, a garden, a man, a woman, and God have to do with my life? I fell asleep over chapter five, which listed the generations from Adam to Noah by name. Convinced I'd never read such an antiquated, boring book again, I returned that Bible to the bookstore and pocketed half the cash I'd shelled out for it.

Since then, I've discovered that Bible study and reading doesn't have to be boring. Creative, thoughtful methods of teaching kids what the Bible is about and how it relates to life abound.[8] The deciding factors for kids, though, are *with whom*, *where*, and *how* the Bible is read.

One of my favorite books is *Jane of Lantern Hill*, the last book written by L. M. Montgomery of *Anne of Green Gables* fame. At the beginning of Jane's story, we discover how the eleven-year-old protagonist feels about the Bible:

> Every night before Jane went to bed, she had to read a chapter in the Bible to grandmother and Aunt Gertrude. There was nothing in the whole twenty-four hours that Jane hated doing more than that. . . . Aunt Gertrude took the huge family Bible, with its heavy silver clasp, from the marble-topped center table and laid it on a little table between the windows. Then she and grandmother sat, one at each end of that table, and Jane sat between them at the side, with Great-grandfather Kennedy scowling down at her from the dim old painting in its heavy, tarnished gilt frame, flanked by the dark blue velvet curtains. . . .
>
> "Turn to the fourteenth chapter of *Exodus*," grandmother would say. The chapter varied every night, of course, but the tone never did. It always rattled Jane so that she generally made a muddle of finding the right place. And grandmother, with the hateful little smile which seemed to say, "so you can't even do this as it should be done," would put out her lean, crepey hand, with its rich old-fashioned rings, and turn to the right place with uncanny precision. . . . Jane would stumble through the chapter, mispronouncing words she knew perfectly well just because she was so nervous.[9]

Fortunately, Jane visits her father halfway through the book and *they* begin reading the Bible together:

> Jane found it did not require a miracle to make her like the Bible. She and dad went to the shore every Sunday afternoon and he read to her from it. Jane loved those Sunday

afternoons. They took their suppers with them and ate them squatted on the sand. . . . She loved the dunes. . . . She loved the music of the winds that whistled along the silvery solitude of the sand-shore. . . . She loved the far dim shores that would be jeweled with home-lights on fine blue evenings. And she loved dad's voice reading the Bible to her. He had a voice that would make anything sound beautiful. . . . And she loved the little comments he made as he read . . . things that made the verses come alive for her. She had never thought that there was anything like that in the Bible.[10]

After reading the Bible with Dad, Jane's response to her required daily dose of Scripture changes, as recounted by Montgomery:

"I should prefer a little more *reverence* in reading the Bible, Victoria," said grandmother. Jane had been reading an old Hebrew war tale as father would have read it, with a trumpet clang of victory in her voice. Grandmother looked at her vindictively. It was plain that reading the Bible was no longer a penance to Jane. She seemed positively to enjoy it. And what could grandmother do about it?[11]

Those reading Scripture at church often mumble or speed their way through the words like Jane before her dad helped her to love the Scriptures. Most churches have lost a vision for prayerful public reading of the Bible:

The Scriptures need to be read in the same spirit in which they were written, and only in that spirit are they to be understood. You will never reach an understanding of Paul until, by close attention to reading him and the application of continual reflection, you imbibe his spirit. You will never arrive at understanding David until by the actual experience you realize what the psalms are about. And so it is with the rest. In every piece of Scripture, real attention is as different from mere reading as friendship is from entertainment, or the love of a friend from a casual greeting.[12]

On the rare Sunday morning when a lector reads the Bible with "real attention," the sensation is akin to the delightful shock of jumping into a cool lake on a steaming day. Whether we read the Bible at church or at home, we're called to employ voice and body, tone and inflection, heart and soul, and thus make it come alive for our hearers the way Jane's dad did.

Family Bible reading can engage our kids in the ancient church traditions of *scholastic lectio*, which allows questions and dispute (the way of knowledge), as well as *monastic lectio* or *lectio divina*, which fosters meditation and prayer (the way of wisdom). The former provides kids with a solid grasp of theology, an understanding of how the canon was formed, and good arguments for the historicity of the Bible. The latter, perhaps, is more important in spiritual formation as it allows the Scriptures to change lives.

The practice of *lectio divina*, or sacred reading, was developed and shared by monastics around their communal table centuries ago. The twelfth-century Carthusian Prior, Guigo II, breaks the process down into four steps: reading, meditation, prayer, and contemplation.[13] We can envision taking these steps with a group of monks, perhaps, but how do we practice *lectio divina* with our kids? Here's one person's suggestion:

Read a short passage in the Bible. (Work your way through either the Gospel of Matthew or Luke; they contain the most stories.) In the course of a short conversation with your child, cover the four basic questions of the *lectio* method: 1) What just happened in the passage we read? (Your child may have questions for you in this part, but don't get hung up on details; some will remain a mystery.) 2) What is this passage saying to you personally? 3) What do you want to say to God based on what we read together? And 4) What does God want to say to or ask of you through this passage and exercise? Show your child the way by sharing your own responses.[14]

*Lectio divina* may or may not be a good fit for you or your kids. But no matter what spiritual discipline you employ, ambassador families must be marked by meditation on the Scripture, allowing it to simmer in our souls so that the lore and law of our land can change us as well as the culture of our posting.

## Fostering Ties to the Community

The second way to instill patriotism in our kids is to connect them to other citizens of the kingdom. Let's face it: this requires regular attendance at worship on Sundays from infancy on. It also comes with involvement in small groups of other Christians, and a commitment to a local church that endures despite that congregation's shortcomings.

"But church is so boring for my kids," parents complain. "It's a chore to drag them here."

Some of the blame rests on churches for this, of course. But as a person who grew up outside the church, I'm amazed that every parent doesn't grab the chance to join a community of faith. Far from our extended family in India, the only adults with whom my sisters and I interacted significantly were our parents. In contrast, I watch my own kids grow up inside a church-based circle of love, blessed by older men and women who pray for them, single "aunts" and "uncles" who notice and celebrate their growth, young adults who teach and encourage them when we're too exhausted to do it.

Even as we acknowledge and accept our kids' boredom, it's okay to be old-fashioned about this one. We're still the parents; *we* decide if our kids go to church or soccer on Sunday mornings as long as they're under our roof, as the timeworn adage goes. Personally, I take heart, noticing that families who hold fast to the priority of church involvement from the start have less trouble bringing the whole family once their kids become teenagers.

Faithfulness in meeting together with other Christians demonstrates that church isn't primarily about what we *get* when we go. Like everything else related to the kingdom of heaven, it's about what we *give*. Check your postchurch conversation on the way home to unveil your focus. By orienting ourselves to gratitude instead of grumbling, we show our kids that diplomats representing Jesus serve a consular role as well—we're trained to serve the needs of kingdom citizens as well as foreigners. Even when bored or tired, the discipline of meeting with other citizens is a nonnegotiable for ambassador families. It's part of the job.

### Cultivating a Love of the King

When we first arrived in the monarchy of Thailand, we noticed that every store and home displayed a picture of the king and queen on the wall, high above the level of the heads of commoners. In movie theaters, people stood in reverence as a montage of the king and his life played on the screen before the previews began. Criticizing or insulting the king or the royal family was a severe offense, punishable with up to fifteen years of imprisonment. Most Thais, however, didn't adore their king because such loyalty was legislated. The fervor of their patriotism was linked to the king's benevolent leadership and to their love for him. (Unfortunately, that particular king is aging fast, and rumor has it that his oldest son is by no means as popular.)

Like the Thai people who are devoted to their king, our kids must develop a deep love and loyalty to our heavenly King. We can't force our children to love Jesus, but we can pray for it to happen, and we can demonstrate a genuine delight in spending time with God. Susana Wesley, for example, used to pull her apron over her head at different times during the week. Her children learned that when this happened, they were to be silent in the kitchen, because Mother was spending time with Jesus again. (I feel better about my own weak spiritual life by imagining a few of Susana's under-the-apron prayer sessions evolving into nice, restful naps.)

My own father, although not a follower of Jesus Christ, taught me much about loving God. He would respond to a beautiful sunset with an outpouring of thanksgiving to the Creator. Tears still pour unheeded down his cheeks when he describes how God delivered and rescued him from a childhood of deprivation in a Bangladeshi village. The ease I feel in expressing tenderness and awe in worship is related directly to my father's open, heartfelt adoration of God. It was rare when Dad didn't bring the subject of his gratitude to God into any one-on-one conversation I had with him as a child. It's still rare today. Likewise, I hope to instill the habit of talking about and to Jesus in my own children's lives.

## Patriots for Christ

When diplomat turns traitor, the offense seems doubly evil. New evidence recently obtained from Russia, for example, reveals that the McCarthy-led outrage against diplomat Lawrence Duggan was justified. Duggan actually did spy for the Soviet Union while representing the United States in Latin America. If Henry Wallace had become president on Roosevelt's death instead of Truman, Duggan might even have been appointed secretary of state. It's hard to read about the shocking betrayal of a high-ranking foreign service officer in an age of terrorism. Even though I'm a staunch advocate of liberty and privacy, I find myself wishing the State Department would require a track record of patriotism from every foreign service applicant.

Patriotism to one's homeland is the only way to ensure the absence of treachery among the diplomatic corps. It can and has motivated ambassadors to lay down their lives in service to their country. As our children grow in their knowledge of Scripture, form bonds of love with other citizens in the community of faith, and become devoted to our King, our hope is that they develop the single-minded patriotism that sustains the finest of ambassadors.

## Focus Story: Consumer Culture

After fifteen years of serving as missionaries in a remote Asian village, the Coles returned to the States with their teenagers to take care of Pete's aging parents. They settled into life in a suburban home down the street from the older set of Coles, and were beginning to feel like the reverse culture shock was wearing off.

One Friday evening after dinner, they stayed around the table to read the Bible and talk, the way they used to in their house on bamboo stilts. "Any topics for family discussion and prayer tonight?" Pete asked, after his wife Tasanee had read the story of Jesus and the miraculous catch of fish.

"I've got one. Can we buy a television?" It was Jeremy, their youngest, a freshman in high school.

"Yeah!" Mary added. "I feel so out of it when kids talk about the shows they watch. We're already like total aliens." She was a junior.

Tasanee shook her head vehemently. "No way. Those shows aren't free, you know. You pay for them by watching the ads—ads which tell you over and over again that you need to have more stuff or to change your appearance to be happy."

The phone rang. "I'll get it!" said Mary, obviously glad to escape the rest of her mother's lecture. She came back looking even more pleased. "Some kids are going to the mall again. They want me to come with them. Isn't that great? We've been praying for Jeremy and I to make friends, and now it's happening!"

Pete frowned. "Why not invite them over here instead? You went to the mall last Friday."

"That's where all the kids hang out, Dad. It's totally safe."

*The stores love it*, Tasanee thought grumpily. Mary had brought home an ugly pair of earrings last weekend. And she'd emptied her wallet on that expensive scarf with a designer logo because "all her friends decided they needed the same one." Tasanee remembered wistfully how Mary used to spend hours teaching the village kids to play hopscotch and other games, or eagerly reading the books her grandparents sent each month. *She hasn't read a book in weeks.*

Jeremy interrupted his mother's depressing train of thought. "Hey, let's get back to the television question," he said. "Can we get one? Oh, and you know the fifty dollars Grandpa gave me for Christmas? Can I use it to buy a Game Boy? Aaron keeps asking me to battle him, so I need my own."

Jeremy had spent some of last year's Christmas money on a bag of rubber balls for the boys in the village. With the rest, he'd bought a wagon for an elderly basket weaver who was getting too old to haul her wares on her back.

Tasanee and Pete exchanged glances. It was happening! Their kids were being lured by consumerism and material-ism—the twin idols of American suburban life. They were feeling the pull, too. Pete, thinking of all the baseball games he'd enjoyed watching with his own Dad, had been trying to convince Tasanee privately that a television could be a gift. Maybe Jeremy would spend more time at home if they bought one. And Tasanee had caught herself thinking that she had "nothing to wear" to church while staring at a closetful of clothes. Short of heading back to the village, was there any way to preserve their family's core values of simplicity, compassion, and generosity?

125

## Put It Into Practice

1. What one practical recommendation would you offer the Coles if they came to you for advice?

2. In the Sermon on the Mount, Jesus pointed out the impossibility of dual citizenship:

   > No one can serve two masters. Either he will hate the one and love the other, or he will be devoted to the one and despise the other. You cannot serve both God and Money. (Matt. 6:24)

   Be on the hunt for any subversive, antimaterialistic trends in pop culture itself that are trying to reform the mainstream's self-indulgence. How will participating in this subversion affect our relationships with friends and neighbors, both inside and outside the church? How might ambassadors of the King help transform culture and rescue others caught in the snare of serving money?

3. Evaluate your own "patriotism." How well versed are you in the lore and law of the land? How strong are your ties to other citizens of the kingdom? How deep and sure is your loyalty to the King? Set some goals for growth in each of these three areas.

## Bringing It Home (for the Family or Small Group)

4. In Janet Tashjian's vaguely Buddhist young adult novel, *The Gospel According to Larry*, the protagonist restricts himself to only seventy-five possessions, including shirts, shoes, keys, books, CDs, and underwear.[15] When Josh acquires or is given something new, his self-imposed code requires him to give something else away. As a family or as individuals, list the seventy-five things you would keep if you submitted to Josh's code. Track your-

selves for a set time and note when you used items that weren't on your list.

5. Some adults practice a double standard when it comes to criticizing the consumerism of our kids' generation. Jonny Baker, who has been involved with youth ministry in London for over fifteen years, wrote an eloquent rant against this:

> [T]he response of many adult Christians . . . is to think how terrible it is that young people are being manipulated by the MTVs and Hollywoods of this world. By implication, the stuff of popular culture (and therefore the world of young people) tends to be viewed very negatively. And the pressure is on youth ministers to protect young people from it.
>
> There are several problems with this. The first is that it fails to recognize that we adult Christians are also living our lives the same way. We are playing the same game! The only difference is that we are making different consumer choices—different music, TV programs, clothes, cars, etc. But we still use these things to construct identity and to associate with people of similar tastes. While it's true that this is sometimes done by purchasing Christian products, it's still just stuff. Stuff that is usually mass-produced, marketed, branded and sold just like everything else. The chances are that others in our church have similar patterns of consumption. But there is nothing inherently wrong in any of this. I'm just amazed at the lack of honesty about it.
>
> Secondly, this view doesn't take into account the ways in which young people actually weave popular culture into their lives to create meaning. It assumes young people are gullible and easily manipulated. In contrast, recent work in cultural studies suggests that audiences often consume in ways very different to what producers intend. I think young people in particular are creative consumers, creating new meanings out of things and subverting those intended by the cultural producers.

...I don't for a minute wish to suggest that we should uncritically embrace consumerism. Clearly, there are very real problems with a materialistic culture. There simply isn't enough stuff to satisfy everyone's desires without the planet teetering over the edge. Not everyone can afford what's in the shops, so there's an increase in poverty and crime. Consumption is usually focused around "me" and perpetuates a selfish approach to life. And ultimately goods don't live up to their promises. You can switch brands and still not know who you are. You can have a life full of things and still feel empty. It's also clear that many materialistic values run counter to those expressed by Jesus in the "beatitudes," his manifesto for an upside-down kingdom.

However, it's time to stop pretending that we (adults) live outside of it judging others (young people) who live inside of it. It's "the water we are all swimming in" and it's time we admitted it. It's time to stop railing against popular culture. By all means, rail against consumerism; but don't just pick on what young people are into.[16]

Take stock of how you have submitted to or resisted the lure of consumerism particular to your generation's culture. Share an example of a success and a failure with the group.

6. What might be missed by others if you didn't go to church? What, if anything, might be missed by God? Name a few things you or your family gains from affiliation with a local congregation and give thanks to God for them.

7. Practice *lectio divina* as a family or small group using Matthew 18:1–9.

8. Write a one-page letter to Jesus telling him of your love and loyalty. Read another person's letter aloud as a prayer of devotion.

# 8

## Savoir-Faire

A diplomat is a man who says you have an open mind instead of telling you that you have a hole in the head.

Unknown[1]

While patriotism to the kingdom of heaven is essential, we also help our kids to develop a quality known in diplomatic circles as *savoir-faire*. The *Encarta World English Dictionary* defines this word as "acting appropriately and adroitly in any situation."[2] Another dictionary describes it as the ability "to say and do the right thing at the right time." The literal French translation is "knowing how to do." *Savoir-faire* (abbreviated in the colloquial as "savvy") enables ambassadors to represent their countries graciously and truthfully in any cultural context.

Roger Axtell, an author who writes frequently about cross-cultural savvy (or lack thereof), tells the story of an American who gave his Japanese counterparts penknives as a parting gift.

Gift giving is an essential part of Japanese culture, but giving a knife to a Japanese man implies you want him to commit suicide.[3] Oops.

In an interview with *Salon*, Axtell described other gesture-related blunders made by the leaders of two powerful countries:

> In 1991, when George Bush [Senior] visited Australia, he did the V for victory sign in the window of his limo—but unfortunately, his hand was the wrong way around. In all the British Commonwealth countries, this is the bird, it means "up yours." So there were pictures of him flipping the bird in all the newspapers.
>
> Boris Yeltsin was sitting next to Barbara Bush at a White House dinner. He turned to his translator and asked, "What does it mean in the United States when a woman puts her foot on a man's foot?"...In Russia, it means she's romantically attracted to the man ... [and] Mrs. Bush had her foot on top of his right then. . . . [As a] joke, [Yeltsin] wrote an inscription on his menu and gave it to Mrs. Bush: "You stepped on my foot, you knew what it meant, and I felt the same way."[4]

I can imagine Barbara Bush laughing hilariously without understanding Yelstin's strange message in the least. Given the lessons she learned from her husband's Australian debacle, I trust she had acquired enough *savoir-faire* to at least chuckle.

Savvy diplomats use communication, courtesy, and camaraderie to build cross-cultural relationships. As our families represent Jesus in the world of pop culture, our goal is to model *savoir-faire* in our own lives and encourage the development of it in our children's lives.

## Communication

How do we communicate with the creators and consumers of popular culture? Earlier in this book, we considered how

Jesus used spoken language to intrigue the Samaritan woman in her spiritual journey. But another part of savvy diplomacy is listening.

We were given two ears and one mouth, as smart alecks like to point out. Ambassadors, missionaries, foreign investors, and development workers are trained with cautionary horror stories about those who ventured cross-culturally without listening to the people. There's the example of the unused well dug by benevolent foreigners who didn't know the witch doctor had cursed that particular site. There's the tale of the missionaries who set up church just like they did back at home and wondered why none of the villagers showed up. If they'd asked, they'd have heard about the bloody battle of independence fought against Western colonial powers. They'd have learned how native Christians were killed because of their association with a "Western" religion.

Father Andrew M. Greeley encourages ambassador families to hear the cries and complaints within pop culture:

> The roots-seeking rock musicians are reflecting a broad cultural discontent as well as articulating and shaping it. If one reads the literature and listens to the music . . . one is almost overwhelmed by their passion for roots. They express one of the most desperate yearnings of modern humankind, a religious and human need which cannot long be denied.[5]

Our kids are better at listening than we are. We're the ones turning it off, switching channels, shutting our ears and minds to the "noise" of pop culture. Developing diplomatic savvy as a family involves a cross-generational give and take—our kids help us to listen, and we help them to discern Greeley's "yearnings of modern humankind."

The Institute for the Study of American Popular Culture publishes *Americana*, a journal dedicated to (what else?) listening to American popular culture. Their goal is to "find the 'voices' that write, play, film, photograph, manufacture, tell, dance, sculpt, paint, and thus explain our American story, our American history."[6] As ambassadors for God in popular culture, we join the Institute in finding voices that explain our story, but we go one step farther and listen for them crying out for God's involvement in that story.

I'm a stereotypical girly-girl recluse whose idea of a hobby is reading books like *Little Women* and *Anne of Green Gables*. Thanks to my preteen sons, I've learned to enjoy the worlds of Marvel Comics, Star Craft, Nintendo, Xtreme Sports, Yu-Gi-Oh, Pokemon, *Jurassic Park*, EA Games, *Jaws*, and *Star Wars*. I know that girls are into these forms of pop culture as well, but most were designed particularly to influence and entertain boys. Listening carefully, I hear the articulation of "masculine" goals—embarking on a hero's quest, courageous, self-sacrificial battle against a diabolical enemy, defense and protection of the weak, the joy of playing in the company of friends. Such themes are echoes of our kingdom's stories, and especially of the greatest quest ever fulfilled—the triumph of our King in his brief sojourn on this planet. As my sons encouraged me to open my mind and ears and *listen*, I began to discern the deep desires within the unfamiliar realm of "boy-dom."

Ambassador families must heed the advice of an unknown quipster: diplomacy is thinking twice before saying nothing. If we withhold our negative comments about pop culture and tune in, our kids, too, might become discerning listeners for the kingdom's sake.

## Courtesy

The second characteristic of *savoir-faire* is courtesy. A good ambassador never condemns the host culture nor assumes the role of a superior critic. Unfortunately, Christians often demonstrate discourteous behavior when it comes to interacting with pop culture—especially with youth culture. "Such trash," we mutter. "So cheesy." How do our kids feel when we grumble incessantly about their generation's expressions of pop culture? Why wouldn't they write off our objections as the stuffiness of an older person who only recognizes the word "hip" when it's followed by "replacement surgery"?

Let's admit it—much of our criticism has nothing to do with religion and everything to do with age. Why is the light rock music station superior to the one that plays rap or hip-hop? It's not. It just suits us better culturally. Listen to the shared and outspoken conviction of faculty in Bowling Green State University's Department of Popular Culture Studies:

> Materials which are genuinely popular, whether we ourselves approve of or enjoy any particular item or genre, are socially and possibly aesthetically significant.[7]

It's common for parents to harbor distaste for youth culture. My own was revealed on a flight from Louisville to Boston. I'd secured an aisle seat toward the front and was looking forward to reading my book in peace. I was hoping I'd have all three seats in the row to myself when a teen dressed in tight black clothes—part Goth, part trash queen—pushed past my knees. She swore as she stumbled into the window seat. Noting her spiky black hair, pale skin, tattoo, and the hook dangling from a pierced lip that accentuated her angry expression, I knew I didn't have to worry about making small talk. This rebel would have nothing to say to a middle-class middle-aged woman like me.

I went back to my book, but as the plane began to gather speed for takeoff, I noticed the sleazy Goth princess hugging herself tightly. I looked over. No way! Yes! This pierced and tattooed alien who'd used the "F-word" instead of "Excuse me" was actually . . . crying. My maternal instincts shifted from neutral into high gear. "What's the matter, sweetheart?" I asked.

"I'm—I'm scared of flying!" she blurted out frantically. She thrust her open hand, green fingernails, skull ring, and all, into the empty seat between us. "Could you hold my hand—just during takeoff and landing?"

I did, of course. She let go only once we were high in the air with the seatbelt sign turned off, and I dried my sweaty palm surreptitiously. My row-mate kept her nose (and hooked lip) plastered against the window and didn't say a word the whole flight. About twenty minutes before we were scheduled to land, a green-tipped open hand plunked down on the empty seat between us. Again I took it, and again she clutched my hand tightly until we reached the gate.

I'll always be thankful for the way that particular traveling companion opened my eyes to see—instead of overlook—the inhabitants of youth culture. Her vulnerability exposed my condemnation and kindled a courtesy that had been lacking in my heart.

Courtesy is expressed in the warm hospitality savvy diplomats extend toward the residents of the host culture. Christians, in contrast, are famous for bans and boycotts of products savored freely outside the church. As ambassador families, we can't be defined by a list of "don't-touches," "don't-tastes," and "don't-handles," as Paul put it in his letter to the Colossians (Col. 2:21, my paraphrase). Sure of our identity as patriots in the kingdom of God, we're free to open homes and minds fearlessly to pop culture instead of slamming the door and locking it. We're supposed to be as "wise as serpents," of course, so we don't invite the pop culture versions of murderers, rapists, and robbers to enter our homes. But we do watch hit movies, read blockbusters, view critically acclaimed off-Broadway shows, visit art galleries, and turn on the radio and listen to a range of stations. We talk about these encounters with our kids, asking positive questions like: "What did you like? Did it remind you of anything we've read about recently in the Bible? Did you discern the presence or the desire for God anywhere?"

Diplomatic courtesy also requires that we respond to overtures of friendship from the host country. Sometimes advances from popular culture toward the church are difficult to recognize as such. In his interview for *Salon*, Robert Axtell describes how he almost missed an opportunity to connect across borders because he didn't understand a particular gesture:

> As I was walking down the street in Jiddah, Saudi Arabia, with a customer who represented millions of dollars worth of business, he reached over and grasped my hand and continued walking down the street, hand-in-hand. . . . I started to sweat. I was lucky—I was so stunned that I didn't let go. In his country, that was a sign of friendship and respect; he was paying me a real compliment by saying I was his friend and it was nothing more than that. If I had pulled away, I'm sure I would have offended him.[8]

Ambassador families notice anything in the world of popular culture hinting at a desire for connection with us or with our King. It's rare, but it does happen—especially now that our communities are being courted as the so-called "untapped evangelical market." Chuck Colson, in his widely read (at least by evangelicals) column Breakpoint, noted the friendship extended toward Christians in the movie *Raising Helen*:

> What's not expected, at least in the movies, is the biggest source of help: the local Lutheran pastor and principal of the kids' school, who becomes Helen's love interest.
>
> True, Pastor Dan Parker is better looking than 99 percent of the clergy you'll ever meet (this is Hollywood, after all). Still, a minister, solid and grounded, is the kind of guy Helen would never have noticed prior to becoming a parent. That makes him a symbol of how becoming a parent changes not only our perspectives but even our perceptions.

135

Director Garry Marshall says that he was drawn to *Raising Helen* largely because of the role of the minister. He noted the negative way that religion and religious people are often portrayed in the media and felt that it was necessary to show that faith and the faithful make positive contributions to our lives.

That may sound obvious to you, but think about the last time you saw a minister as the hero, or at least as an admirable lead, on the big screen. A man wearing a collar is usually, at best, an ineffectual dolt or, at worst, a rigid fanatic and the villain. According to Marshall, in *Raising Helen*, the pastor's presence is intended to reassure the audience that Helen and the three kids are going to be all right.[9]

Now that's a courteous response to a Hollywood flick, especially one with a director lacking "Christian" credentials. I even read the review aloud so my movie-loving kids could hear an evangelical leader rave instead of rant about their favorite realm of pop culture.

## Camaraderie

Camaraderie across cultures is built through shared experiences. My parents arrived in America when they were middle-aged. They socialized mainly with other Bengalis, and their only club or community involvement was in the regional Bengali association. This meant they had few American friends. But then a neighbor invited my mom to walk with her on a regular basis. Trust grew, and they began discussing the ups and downs of their lives. That single shared activity with a friend equipped my mom to feel at home in America more than a hundred seminars on how to be an American. It's the same way with the citizens of popular culture—we might offer dozens of classes and programs inside the hallowed halls of our churches, but they'll learn much more about our King by sharing experiences with us on common ground.

Basically, this means just doing stuff together. Hang. Relax. Chill. Play. Chat. A group of young adults in our church enjoy volleyball regularly at a gym, for example, opening up their games to anybody in the neighborhood. Various members in my women's Bible study participate in community quilting groups, choral societies, or book groups. An elder in our church coaches soccer teams for kids in his community. I enjoy the company of the other members in my writer's group as we discuss how to craft stories for young readers. In all of these contexts, ambassadors for the kingdom of God are interacting with people who have little or no familiarity with the Bible or the ways of our King.

Another key way to build camaraderie is by sharing laughter. Savvy diplomats must have a sense of humor, especially in an era of strained foreign relations. Karl Gruber, Austrian foreign minister and Austrian ambassador to the United States, Spain, Switzerland, and West Germany, remembers an incident when a diplomat's sense of humor broke the ice:

> A good diplomat . . . should always have some remarks ready to ease tension once negotiations get near a breaking point. One example that comes to mind involves a negotiation in which everything went wrong. (It happened to involve agrarian exchanges in Central Europe, a subject that is always tough and intractable). One of the negotiators had a long beard, and his stolid demeanor did not augur well for a successful outcome. His counterpart finally said: Before we part, I have one more question. When you go to sleep at night, do you tuck your beard under the covers or do you leave it above them? There was laughter all around, and for the first time the patriarch allowed a smile to crease his lips.[10]

A sense of humor might help evangelicals disentangle ourselves from the messy "culture wars" that have hindered diplomacy over the past decade or two. A few ambassadors, thankfully, are beginning to communicate the lore of our kingdom in a winsome, self-deprecatory, even downright funny voice.

Last, but not least, to build camaraderie where animosity has divided cultures, the savvy ambassador must take pleasure in the products of that host country. Relishing what the locals consider their specialty is a delightful manifestation of diplomatic *savoir-faire*.

When my husband arrived in my grandfather's home as the first foreign son-in-law ever to cross that threshold, I was nervous to say the least. My aunts were wearing their best sarees, and my uncles had spared no expense on the lavish spread that accompanied our afternoon tea. I noticed the sticky, juicy *rasgallah* floating in thick syrup—a traditional Bengali sweet that most Americans couldn't stomach.

My uncle picked up the bowl. "Take," he commanded politely, as Indian men do, sluicing one round white ball on Rob's plate. *Surely he'll manage to finish one*, I thought, practically wringing my hands as I watched.

Bravely, Rob forked the soggy sphere into his mouth. I held my breath as he chewed diligently. Then his face lit up. "Hey, this is good!" he said, his voice ringing with unmistakable sincerity. Everybody beamed as he picked up the bowl and heaped three more *rasgallah*s onto his plate.

"He's such a nice boy," my aunts confided in the kitchen.

My grandfather pronounced his blessing. "Welcome to our family, my son," he said. The "in-law" part of the title had vanished along with the *rasgallah*s.

When we moved to New England, it took us a bit longer to figure out how to bond with the locals. My first clue came when a pair of dowagers adorned in flowery swim caps passed me in the locker room at the gym.

One of them sighed and shook her petal-covered head. "We got so close!" she muttered.

"Those horrible Yankees," the other responded, just as glumly.

Red Sox fever. It permeates New England like a palpable aura when the Sox get anywhere close to the playoffs. Rooting for the Sox binds New Englanders more tightly than griping about snow. Despite my identity as a bookworm who never watched sports (other than the Olympics and an occasional Wimbledon finals), even I got caught up in it. Would Trot Nixon's injury keep him out of the game? Would Jason Varitek sign on to play another season? I stayed up with my husband past midnight more than once watching nine long innings of baseball, flummoxed that I actually found this pastime enjoyable. But it was more than the baseball that was captivating us; it was the communal bonding that was helping our family to feel at home in this new place.

Camaraderie. Courtesy. Communication. How to cultivate savvy diplomacy in the next generation of ambassadors representing the kingdom of God? Like Red Sox fever in New England, *savoir-faire* is better caught than taught.


## Focus Story: Sports

Devon glanced up into the bleachers and spotted his father's face. *Dad's about to lose it,* he thought. *10–9–8–7 . . .*

"Hey Ref! You blind? The guy fouled him from behind." Devon's tall, handsome father was standing, cupping his hands around his mouth to make sure he could be heard on the gym floor.

Devon's teammate elbowed him. "There goes your dad again. He's sort of intense, dude."

"Yeah, Dev. He preach as loud as he yells?" The guys on the bench laughed uneasily.

Devon shrugged. "He's into it is all. Nothing wrong with that."

But there was. Dad was the minister of the largest church in town, and usually as sweet as apple pie. Except for when he was around sports. A competitive streak a mile wide ran through Dad's soul, and no matter what game he was playing or watching, *his* team had to win. Even if he had to shout and scream at them and everybody else to make it happen.

Devon was glad he was on the bench. When he was out on the court, his Dad got even more riled up. Mom got so embarrassed, she didn't even come to the games any more. The funny thing was, none of the elders at church seemed to mind Dad's outbursts; in fact, one of them had told Devon they made Dad easier to be around, more like "one of them" instead of the previous preacher who'd been too "holy" to show that he cared about a game.

Devon thought back to all the Little League baseball games, basketball games, and track meets where Dad had lost his cool. Devon used to be the star athlete in every one of those sports. But bit by bit, he'd started pulling back from playing to relieve some of the stress on his father. He didn't like to see that vein popping out on Dad's temple. *He's gonna die of a stroke watching a game*, Devon thought, shaking his head as Dad began screaming again.

## Put It into Practice

1. We encourage our kids to join leagues and teams, driving them hither and yon to play sports. As fans, we spend money and time unstintingly to support our team. But some pop culture watchers feel that our love of sports borders on idolatry. T. M. Moore writes:

> The culture of sports has penetrated the life of the evangelical community, threatening the sanctity of the day of rest, inhibiting the church's ability to equip and

send its members for ministry, and undermining other aspects of its distinctiveness as a subculture in American society. Yet, for the most part, evangelicals seem hardly troubled by this—certainly not as much as many of them are about the presence of pop music in the church. The evangelical community . . . is so enamored of the beauty and virility of this intruder that it does not sense the threat to its distinctiveness as a community.[11]

Where and how should a Christian draw the line when it comes to competitiveness in play, participation in sports, and support of a team?

2. Some Christians feel that boxing, professional football, wrestling, and other contact sports celebrate and promote violence to the point of sin. Is there any sporting activity you wouldn't watch or participate in as a follower of Jesus? Why or why not? Make a case showing how participation in your favorite athletic activity promotes the values of the kingdom of God.

3. Evaluate your diplomatic *savoir-faire*. What's a recent positive comment you made about something in youth culture? Think of a couple of books that weren't written by Christians and yet affected you deeply. What product of pop culture have you thoroughly enjoyed as a gift from God?

## Bringing It Home (for the Family or Small Group)

4. Do you have any suggestions or advice for Devon and/ or his father? (Suggestion: Let the younger generation answer first.)

5. In his letter to the Ephesians, Paul admonishes followers of Jesus to avoid "coarse joking" (Eph. 5:4). Brainstorm a list of the top five or ten colloquial words (excluding obscenities) that might turn up in a "coarse" joke. As you

watch television, listen to the radio, surf the Net, walk in the mall, or interact at school or at work, note a few things that made people laugh. Were any words on your list involved? Did you laugh when everybody else did? Why or why not? (If you found the joke online or in a book, you might have been the only one laughing.)

6. What do you do on your own for fun? How do you have fun with friends your age? Parents: For a half-hour this week, do what your kid does for fun on his or her own. Kids: If possible, try what your mom or dad considers "fun" for a half-hour this week. If possible (and legal), convince a couple of peers to try the group activity enjoyed by the other generation.

# 9

## Tenacity

A diplomat's life is made up of three ingredients: protocol, Geritol, and alcohol.

Adlai E. Stevenson[1]

Will a foreign service officer persevere through a lifetime of diplomatic service? A slew of recent gory headlines make one wonder why anybody would want to:

Turkish diplomats attacked by Armenian terrorists. Bomb attack on the US Embassy in Bogota, Colombia. Japanese diplomats murdered in Iraq. Ten Iranian diplomats slaughtered when Taliban guards enter the Iranian Consulate in Mazar-e Sharif. Indonesian terror group targets Australian diplomats.

The children of diplomats are not exempt from threatening situations:

In the pastoral setting of the [U.S.] Foreign Service Institute's grounds in Arlington, Va., you'll find children outside during the summer months, standing in a circle and screaming at the top of their lungs. This is no cause for alarm—they are demonstrating their knowledge of what to do if in a dangerous situation, something they've learned by participating in the Youth Security Overseas Seminar.[2]

Most career foreign service officers are required to serve in a hardship posting. They serve their governments far from the comforts and security of home, perhaps daily interacting with people who hate them because of their nationality. The Samaria of pop culture, as described in chapter 2, can be such a hostile environment for diplomats representing the kingdom of God. Our faith is more likely to survive unscathed and sustain us for the long haul if we take the time to develop a clear-eyed patriotism and the *savoir-faire* of maturity. Children may not be ready for such a challenging posting, especially younger ones. They need tenacity to persevere through the challenging years ahead as diplomats. In tough situations, they need to know how to find a circle of other expatriates and scream for help.

How do you encourage staying power among your diplomatic corps? You keep or bring them home for a while for the purpose of more training. After starting his job as U.S. Secretary of State, Colin Powell was concerned that many senior officers had received almost no training since they joined the service and lacked leadership skills. He decided to make sure that they knew "how to take care of people" and "how to accomplish a mission."[3] Beyond training, state departments and foreign offices also encourage diplomats to take regular "R & R" excursions to safer places. And as much as is possible, home governments protect and shield their public servants who are dwelling in foreign places.

**Delay Deployment or Require Evacuation**

Young children live in a dualistic world of black and white, good and evil, right and wrong. It takes maturity to understand the nuances of mixed motive in the minds of complex people. The producers of pop culture often weave together threads of good and evil, or intermingle themes of darkness and light to form patterns that are difficult for children to discern. (Addendum: I'm a grown-up, and usually I don't get it.)

When our boys were younger, we restricted their consumption of pop culture products that we felt were beyond their capacity to digest. I'd learned as a teacher that the stricter you are in the early part of the academic year, the better kids respond when you relax and loosen up later. Seasoned parents advised us that the same principle holds true in the family. We didn't watch any television at home until they were eleven, for example. We did use a VCR or DVD to watch movies together on Friday nights, but we sought to hold off on the more subversive, powerful influence of commercials. (This policy was easy to enforce because we lived overseas until the boys were seven and then in places where television reception didn't come for free.) We're slow in letting them watch movies that their peers seem to be enjoying without any parental hindrance. We restrict their access to the Internet with filters and time limits. In short, even though we're a family committed to representing Christ in pop culture, we didn't let them travel there for years.

Our pace in sending them out might be different from yours. In fact, it probably is. The wise person who penned the biblical book of Proverbs knew that parents should train up their children in the unique "way *he* [or *she*] should go," not enforce the timing and regulations that work for another person's child (Prov. 22:6). A proactive parent keeps a careful eye on each child's mind, heart, and soul to discern when to keep them within the protection of a "homeland" setting, when

145

to accompany them into the host country of pop culture, and when to let them venture out alone.

Listen to the observations of a comparatively young pop culture watcher (aged thirty-one at the time of writing this article) whose views about a particular cable channel changed over time:

> Maybe I've lost touch now that I've reached full adulthood. Maybe I just can't bridge the generation gap anymore. But to see the shows that aired made me absolutely convinced that in no way, shape or form would I ever want to go back to being a teenager again. It's too rough out there.
>
> The first show was called *Becoming*. In this show, teenagers are selected to become one of their favorite artists. They get dressed up like someone else, then dance someone else's moves and shoot someone else's video. Sounds pretty harmless all in all, right? Wrong. Instead of taking the time to encourage these teens to find their own way and create their own unique styles, MTV tells kids that they should aspire to be like Sisqo.
>
> Now . . . it gets worse.
>
> After *Becoming* came another show called something like *Real Life Stories: The Trials and Tribulations of Today's Youth*. In this show, we saw two twenty-year-old girls, best friends, whose greatest aspirations were to "be in Playboy, and, I dunno, get a boyfriend, I guess." One was getting her nose done, and the other was getting her thighs flattened out. They both had their breasts ridiculously enlarged and were pondering further procedures.
>
> Then there was Brad . . . I believe he was a nineteen-year-old. He was going to have, get this, calf implants. Instead of just working out a little more or eating a few more protein shakes a week, he decided to go under the knife and cut out the middleman. . . .
>
> Then came the coup de grace: *Dismissed*. In this show, either a man or a woman goes out on a date with two members of the opposite sex, who in turn do their best to seduce and woo and ultimately not be "the one who gets dismissed." Now this

is not *Blind Date* or *Change of Heart* where you're dealing with working, tax-paying adults who are usually at least twenty-five and out of college. MTV, sticking to its demographic, uses eighteen- and nineteen-year-olds to "keep it real." What follows is two young girls trying to out-do each other at being the sluttiest or raciest bimbo in the dorm, or the two of them almost scratching each other's eyes out with catty remarks and evil innuendo. Eventually, predictably, the boy chooses the girl with the biggest breasts.

Perhaps I've gone stale. Or perhaps I've just grown up. Regardless, I'm recognizing the generation gap for the first time in my life . . . from the *other* side.

After numerous years of debauchery and a "nothing but fun" attitude, I have grown to appreciate character, moral fiber, adherence to convictions. It makes me quite sad to see what today's teenagers are exposed to at such a young, difficult age. The damage to their psyches overwhelms and upsets mine, but as long as MTV is making a profit. . . . And I thought things were tough way back when.[4]

I was struck by how a few years of maturity changed the author's perspective. With our children, too, a bit more time might be required before they're able to see a particular pop culture product clearly.

Metaphors might help parents explain what seem like severely restrictive policies to our kids. I've tried an amusement park image: "Remember when we went to Disneyland and we rode the kiddie rides first, working our way up until we were ready for Space Mountain? We had such a blast that day, didn't we? But then we went again, and this time we rode Space Mountain first, remember? All the other rides seemed boring in comparison, so the rest of that day wasn't as fun. It's the same thing with entertainment. We want to give you a chance to enjoy the stuff you're just old enough for now instead of rushing you ahead so that this stuff feels tame in comparison."

Did they get it? Who knows? They grumbled, but that's inevitable in parenting. They needed to deepen their patriotism to the kingdom of God and develop the savvy to negotiate a confusing world. It was our job to make sure they had enough time to go through this developmental process.

If our kids are already immersed in popular culture over their heads, it may be time for an evacuation. Evacuations are costly and stressful, but they save expatriate lives. Ambassador Peggy Blackford, for example, authorized a mandatory evacuation for American staff to leave Guinea-Bissau during a coup in 1998. Every American in the capital city rushed to the safety of the embassy, except for seventeen Peace Corps workers who lived outside the capital and had to be airlifted one by one from villages. After the last young, terrified volunteer escaped unscathed on June 13, Blackford describes what happened to the remaining diplomatic staff on the following day:

> [We] drove to an isolated dock where we were picked up by a dinghy from a small tanker. Each of us boarded with a cat or two in one hand and a change of clothes in the other. . . . We lost almost all our prized possessions, yet we were the lucky ones.[5]

If our kids are enmeshed in aspects of popular culture that are "double-d" (dangerous and destructive in school-playground jargon), it may be time for a mandatory evacuation. We can get rid of Internet access in the home for the sake of the child caught in the snare of pornography, for example. This means enduring a cost to ourselves also, but if we really love our kids, isn't it worth the inconvenience?

One of my favorite conversations in *The Fellowship of the Ring*, book 2 of the Lord of the Rings trilogy by J. R. R. Tolkien, takes place when the questing company of men, elf, dwarf, and hobbits stumbles into the lovely Wood of the Lady—Lothlorien. The elves guarding this sanctuary insist that Gimli the dwarf must wear a blindfold to enter their land; a history of enmity between elves and dwarves prevents them from trusting him. Furious, Gimli refuses to submit to the indignity of this restriction and insists that Legolas the elf must also be blindfolded. Angry in turn, Legolas refuses to walk blindly into a land of his people. Aragorn (the archetypical hero of every woman's dreams) intervenes. He decides that all six of them—men, hobbits, dwarf, *and* elf—will be blindfolded as they journey through beautiful Lothlorien. This self-denial on his part earns the cooperation of both Gimli and Legolas, and extinguishes the simmering bitterness between them. If only we parents could be as noble about restricting *our* access to the pop-culture equivalents of lovely Lothlorien on behalf of our wards!

We may have to pay even higher prices to evacuate our kids. A friend pulled her at-risk daughter out of school and taught her at home for a year, for example. The family had to forgo many comforts and luxuries they'd taken for granted because Mom wasn't able to earn any money that year. Mom also lost her place in the job promotion queue. Other parents are quick to seek counseling for a son or daughter at the first hint of any self-destructive behaviors, paying the emotional and relational price of unwanted interventions instead of avoiding confrontation. In desperate scenarios, a few parents are brave enough to quit comfortable jobs and move closer to the help of extended family or friends. Costly, painful, and stressful though they may be, mandatory evacuations may save vulnerable children from destruction.

## Rest and Refreshment

"I'm heading to Sydney for some R & R. Where are you headed?"

"We're spending a week in the Maldives. Can't wait."

We'd overhear conversations like this almost every weekend at the American Club in Dhaka. Diplomats often took breaks from the stress of urban life in a poor, overcrowded Muslim country. They'd head off to tropical islands, tourist destinations, or any place with a Barnes & Noble, Starbucks, and the inimitable Golden Arches that reminded them of home. To survive a hardship posting, many of them considered these "R & R" excursions a necessity as opposed to a luxury.

A diplomat friend explained the general philosophy of R & R from his post in South Asia: "The State Department pays for the travel, though not per diem and accommodations. In general terms, an officer would likely get two R & R trips in a three-year tour. It depends on hardship level though. I think officers serving in Iraq, for instance, get three in one year. Most people assume that it will be taken from particularly rough posts. I've never known anyone who didn't take it in some form or another."

In the same way, ambassador families sent by the King into pop culture need frequent breaks. We need occasional fasts, periodic retreats, and regular Sabbath days away from the adrenaline, static, and neon of our host country.

*Fasts* promote creativity and strengthen weak areas of the soul. I use my laptop every day to correspond, plan appointments and trips, research issues affecting our family, interact with other people's ideas, read the news, and, of course, write. Sometimes, though, it feels like my laptop and I are becoming one. Even as I'm setting rules and limits on "screen and plug" time for the boys, I'm aware of my own need to set apart time for a fast.

Fasts from pop culture work best in tandem. A few parents in our school district, for example, organized a community-wide "unplugged" week. At first, the kids in the neighborhood, including ours, complained vigorously. "We're bo-o-o-red," the mantra of a prosperous childhood, was heard in every home, but their boredom soon became fertile soil for invention. By the second day, most of them were engrossed in jointly created games and activities, arguing over rules and breaches of conduct, learning how to compromise and negotiate and resolve.

While fasting, we need to recall that God never intended us to switch off to feel righteous or to look down on others we label as less "spiritual." ("We *never* let *our* kids watch television, *they* always read *books*.") A true fast is described beautifully in Isaiah 58:

> Is not this the kind of fasting I have chosen:
> to loose the chains of injustice
>     and untie the cords of the yoke,
> to set the oppressed free
>     and break every yoke?
> Is it not to share your food with the hungry
>     and to provide the poor wanderer with shelter—
> when you see the naked, to clothe him,
>     and not to turn away from your own flesh and blood?
> Then your light will break forth like the dawn,
>     and your healing will quickly appear;
> then your righteousness will go before you,
>     and the glory of the LORD will be your rear guard.
> Then you will call, and the LORD will answer;
>     you will cry for help, and he will say: Here am I.
>
> If you do away with the yoke of oppression,
>     with the pointing finger and malicious talk,
> and if you spend yourselves in behalf of the hungry
>     and satisfy the needs of the oppressed,
> then your light will rise in the darkness,
>     and your night will become like the noonday.
> The LORD will guide you always;
>     he will satisfy your needs in a sun-scorched land
>     and will strengthen your frame.
> You will be like a well-watered garden,
>     like a spring whose waters never fail.

151

> Your people will rebuild the ancient ruins
>     and will raise up the age-old foundations;
> you will be called Repairer of Broken Walls,
>     Restorer of Streets with Dwellings. (Isa. 58:7–12)

These verses penned by the prophet Isaiah describe the incredible contribution God's people can make through fasts that allow a focus on service and relationship. Fasts from the world of techno-entertainment free up time to serve the poor and nourish relationships with "flesh and blood." Volunteer service, visits to and from friends and relatives, and family vacations that allow us to enjoy different cultural or natural scenery provide appropriate time away from screens and plugs. For the weary traveler through deserts of Samaria, our unexpected company will feel like the cool shade of a magnolia tree. We'll be given the ability to repair and restore a "world of broken walls" and "streets without dwellings"—popular culture's most dangerous, lonely places. What breathtaking promises!

*Retreats* are another type of R & R that build the tenacity of an ambassador family. While a fast takes us away from screens and plugs to become involved in alternative activities, a retreat is a break taken only for prayer and spiritual renewal. Christian camps and conference centers abound with opportunities for reflection and growth. A couple at our church, for example, raised three kids whose faith survived and even thrived in a relatively hostile public school environment. They firmly believe that a summer of Bible study, friendships, and worship at a Christian camp helped their children fuel up spiritually before every school year. In North America, scholarships and donations sometimes make camping or retreats a possibility for even low-income families.[6]

The third type of R & R takes place once a week: keeping the *Sabbath* day.

> If you keep your feet from breaking the Sabbath
>     and from doing as you please on my holy day,

if you call the Sabbath a delight
    and the LORD's holy day honorable,
and if you honor it by not going your own way
    and not doing as you please or speaking idle words,
then you will find your joy in the LORD,
    and I will cause you to ride on the heights of the land
and to feast on the inheritance of your father Jacob. (Isa.
    58:13–14)

Our family tries to keep Sundays unplugged. After church, we read, play games, take naps, spend time with friends and neighbors, or simply rest in preparation for a week of activity. Our good intentions don't always come to fruition (especially if the Red Sox are playing), but we try our best to set apart Sundays as a time to enjoy different types of activities. Sometimes, we light a candle during Saturday night supper and begin the Sabbath rest as the sun sets.

When the boys were young, I tried to convince them to take Sunday afternoon walks or hikes in quiet, scenic places. One of Wendell Berry's poems describes what the soul experiences on a walk:

> What is the way to the woods, how do you go there?
> By climbing up through the six days' field,
> kept in all the body's years, the body's
> sorrow, weariness, and joy. By passing through
> the narrow gate on the far side of that field
> where the pasture grass of the body's life gives way
> to the high, original standing of the trees.
> By coming into the shadow, the shadow
> of the grace of the strait way's ending,
> the shadow of the mercy of light.
>
> Why must the gate be narrow?
> Because you cannot pass beyond it burdened.
> To come into the woods you must leave behind

the six days' world, all of it, all of its plans and hopes.
You must come without weapon or tool, alone,
expecting nothing, remembering nothing,
into the ease of sight, the brotherhood of eye and leaf.[7]

A Sunday without plugging into the "weapons or tools" of popular culture provides the ease of sight we need to return to Wendell Berry's field. But convincing my kids of this took a lot of negotiating. Their idea of a day in the great outdoors was spending time at an amusement park, replete with shrill screams, sweaty crowds, and high-speed whiplash-creating machines. Riding a roller coaster was the only family activity that effortlessly lured them out of the house. After all, why go outside? The exciting stuff happened inside, like destroying warlords at the computer or watching yet another action-adventure movie.

I had to face the truth: my twenty-first-century–children were addicted to human-made adrenaline. Could they ever be thrilled by the beauty of nature? Their view of nature was fundamentally different from mine. I saw rivers carving ancient paths through a deepening canyon. They pictured themselves "canyoneering," or hurling their bodies into the speed of the white water. I saw a high, curved rock jutting out like a sentinel over a lake. They saw a prime spot for bungee jumping. I watched the waves curl into the shore, enjoying the crash and splendor of the ocean's relentless approach. They checked out the surf and wondered how awesome it would be to hang ten on a board.

On a trip to Mammoth Lakes in California, I gazed up at the steep, snow-covered slopes, wondering if they resented being used for the thrills, chills, and spills of skiing and snowboarding. *Was anybody in awe of nature any more?* I thought. *Was our kids' generation so overentertained and thrill-saturated they couldn't grasp the majesty of nature without exploiting it for adrenaline?*

My family grew weary of my grumbling. "Okay, okay, Mom," my son said. "We'll go on a walk with you. But you have to learn to ski with us."

Me? A middle-aged immigrant designed to live in the tropics? Learn to ski? I was doomed, destined to be a scared, cold, and battered first-timer. Would it be worth it? I gritted my teeth and agreed.

We set out on a short, three-mile hike through Inyo National Forest. Snow had fallen lightly through the night, but it wasn't too deep on the trail. We walked through a forest of frosted evergreens, and I recited a few lines from Robert Frost's familiar poem, "Stopping By the Woods On a Snowy Evening." "The woods are lovely, dark and deep. But I have promises to keep, and miles to go before I sleep. And miles to go before I sleep."

After that, even I knew enough to stay quiet, apart from a word or two of encouragement. We trudged uphill, climbing to the rim between two huge craters. When we reached the top, flushed and breathless with accomplishment, we looked back across the silent, snowy valley. The sun was low in the winter sky, and the last light sparkled on the icy green ponds deep in the bowl of each crater.

In the stillness, the holiness was tangible; the forest had become a cathedral. Our boys' eyes were shining, and I knew they were as thrilled as we were.

After that day, we tried to hike or walk together on Sunday afternoons. The kids grumbled a bit at the start, but after about twenty minutes, the solitude of the countryside wove its familiar spell. I could see their threshold for excitement begin to come down.

"Look, Dad!" one of them called in a low voice. We watched, spellbound, as a pair of deer leapt across a meadow.

"Shhh, Mom," another said, interrupting our conversation. I obeyed, and we listened to the song of a waterfall spilling into a river.

Of course, the give and take between the generations required me to widen my horizons when it came to being thrilled. In return for their company on my Sunday walks, I accept their invitations on other days of the week. I make my way down the bunny slopes and hurtle through the air on death-defying roller coasters, screaming at the top of my lungs the whole way. All in all, it's a good bargain for the whole family.

**Protection and Defense**

After the bombing of their consulate in Istanbul, the British government took decisive action. They moved diplomats away from city centers to various residential areas in the outskirts in Yemen, Uganda, and Indonesia. Embassy staff in Algiers operated out of the Hilton Hotel because their office was seen as vulnerable to attack from militants. Baghdad and Riyadh, the two High Commission (Embassy) locales considered to be most at risk of attack, were heavily protected with armed guards, security cameras, gates, and checkpoints.

America also tries to protect her diplomatic corps, but despite the State Department's best efforts, over seventy U.S. foreign service officers have died in the line of duty in the past twenty years, with fifty-seven of those in the last decade. Over the last half-century, more ambassadors than generals have been killed in service to the United States.

Service to your home country is costly. As with anything worthwhile, risks are involved in accepting a diplomatic assignment. It's natural that we're hesitant to put our kids in the line of fire—we expend so much time and energy trying to save their lives and nurture their faith. Will they survive in a culture that seems to grow more dangerous every decade?

Jesus spoke of sending his disciples out "like lambs among wolves" (Luke 10:3), which is how we often feel when they are exposed to the world of pop culture. How did Jesus deal with his concerns? By crying out to God for the protection of his "children" (see John 17). He asked that God would keep them clean by the truth of the Word as they remained in the world. The best defense, according to our Master, is prayer, especially when we know that the Enemy is out there prowling!

As we lead our kids into the world of pop culture, we can delay their ventures into that world until they're ready, evacuate them in case of emergency, provide regular R & R, and provide vigilant defense and protection through prayer. The end result, if all goes well, is that they'll develop the tenacity to represent Jesus for a lifetime.

### Focus Story: Television

Violence, gratuitous and ubiquitous. Sex, abused and misused. Stereotypes, blatant and subliminal. After an hour of watching prime time with her channel-surfing sixteen-year-old, Jane felt like hurling the television out the window.

"How can you stand watching this stuff?" she asked Sean instead. "It's been blaring since you came home from work. That's three hours ago."

"I had a hard day. This is how I relax."

"But the shows are so trashy, Sean. It's such a waste of time."

Her son gave an exaggerated sigh that made *him* sound like the parent. "Look, Mom. I'm not going to jump into bed with the first girl—or guy—I see. I don't think only white, middle-class people populate the world. And I'm not going to go nuts and beat someone to death."

Jane had to grin. In the intense relationship shared by a single parent and an only child, she and Sean had developed the uncanny knack of reading each other's minds. "But it does affect you," she said. "It has to. What goes in comes out. You usually only watch about two hours or so a day, right?"

"Sometimes less, sometimes more. But so what? Your generation thinks that television is some kind of powerful demon that programs and controls our minds or something. But it doesn't have that much power. I've got the remote, remember? I'm in charge."

"Then how come sometimes you seem so depressed after watching? Or irritated? Or even more tired than when you started?"

"I do not."

"Do too."

"Not."

"Do."

Jane grabbed a pillow, and Sean ducked. The screen flickered unnoticed in the background as Sean leaped from couch to chair to avoid getting pummeled by his mother.

"You're so violent, Mom," he goaded, grabbing a coffee table book to use as a shield. "Been watching too much prime time lately?"

Jane groaned and dropped her weapon. Sean was sixteen, and he worked hard at his part-time job after school. He did need to relax, and paying for cable kept him home, out of trouble. Or did it? Maybe she was keeping him out of the proverbial frying pan and tossing him in the fire. He was still under her roof; still in her care. Should she make a last-ditch effort to limit his television use?

**Put It into Practice**

1. When it comes to watching television, do you agree more with Sean or with Jane? How would you handle Sean's television habit if you were Jane?

2. Read the following quote:

   [We] Asians are seen as standouts at being quiet sidekicks,

making sushi, studying, tinkering with circuit boards, cleaning teeth and doing laundry. We are seen as constitutionally incapable of excelling at basketball, lawyering, sending audiences rolling in the aisles with uncontrolled laughter, seducing virtuous but incredibly sexy women, fighting with cool resourcefulness against astronomical odds—well-oiled pecs and biceps glistening with sexy sweat—to save the world from being blown up by cackling evil geniuses. . . . All too often, we *are* the cackling evil geniuses.[8]

As you watch television, note how many ethnic minorities you see portrayed in shows and in commercials. What are their roles? Do those roles make or break a stereotype?

3. Read this still-apropos excerpt of an article written a few years ago:

Red and gold wrapping paper littered the living room floor. Stocking chocolate smudges stained the velvet couch. Aromas of turkey and my southern mother's favorite, baked oyster stuffing, floated through the air. Only one Christmas gift remained, a small rectangle for my eight-year-old niece. She tore off the wrapping paper and what to her wondering eyes did appear . . . a concert videotape of Britney Spears.

Slipping it into the VCR, she settled down next to me in the overstuffed armchair. Within mere seconds, she was up off the chair swiveling, grinding, and pulsating along with the teen icon. But the sexually explicit body movements were not the end of it. In my little niece's dark brown eyes, I could see the reflection of Britney Spears. Tan, naked Britney Spears.

Here, at this moment, my niece was learning one of her first lessons about the cult of white female beauty. Be tan; plump up your boobs; be super skinny; and show as much of your skin as possible. How stung I was watching her knowing that this lesson, arranging oneself for the benefit of the male gaze, not only has the power profoundly, permanently, persistently to damage a woman's physical health but it has the power profoundly, permanently, persistently to damage a woman's spiritual and psychological health as well.[9]

Does the portrayal of women in this way also damage men spiritually and psychologically? Straight men, and especially straight fathers, are often caricatured on television as bumbling idiots without a clue about women or style. As you watch prime-time shows and especially sit-coms, discern the ways women and men are stereotyped and they way they interact. What assumptions about femininity and masculinity are made?

4. David Grossman, author of *Stop Teaching Our Kids to Kill* (see appendix), makes the following argument:

Violence is like the nicotine in cigarettes. The reason why the media has to pump ever more violence into us is because we've built up a tolerance. In order to get the same high, we need ever-higher levels. . . . [T]he television industry has gained its market share through an addictive and toxic ingredient.[10]

Do you agree or disagree? Do you sense any numbness in your own psyche toward violence?

5. A recent trend in movies and television is violence perpetrated against women. Bob Smithouser of Focus on the Family's *Plugged In* editorialized about this issue:

The leading ladies in today's action films are buff, soulless and quick to put a hurt on guys who underestimate them. But I'm troubled by the number of high-profile flicks of late that have featured muscle-bound hunks and doe-eyed Amazons beating the daylights out of each other. . . .

Terminator 3's Arnold Schwarzenegger met his match in the form of a marauding fembot played by blonde bombshell Kristanna Loken. One unsettling knock-down, drag-out levels a rest room. *Entertainment Weekly* claims Schwarzenegger cracked a mischievous smile when he said, "As we were rehearsing, I saw this toilet bowl. How many times do you get away with this—to take a woman, grab her upside down, and bury her face in a toilet bowl?" . . . The U.S Department of Justice reports that most victims of domestic violence are women ages 16–24. It's the number-1 cause of emergency room visits among females.[11]

Does this violence against women in the media contribute to or simply reflect what's taking place in the culture?

## Bringing It Home (for the Family or Small Group)

6. Is your family "delaying deployment" into any realm of popular culture (i.e., filters, rules, limits)? Why or why not? Do you agree with this strategy? How might this delay affect your ability to shape culture, either positively or negatively?

7. If you became overwhelmed and entangled in a dangerous aspect of pop culture (pornography, drugs, anorexia, cutting), what would you want each of your closest friends or relatives to do?

8. Which of the R & R opportunities (fasts, retreats, Sabbath days) described in this chapter have worked or might work for your family? Why? How would they help your family fulfill your calling as ambassadors to pop culture?

9. If you don't practice this already, set aside the coming Sunday as a Sabbath from the world of screens and

plugs (computers, televisions, movies, radio, gaming). Take a walk together in a peaceful setting. Discuss the experience during your next small group time. Did taking a rest from pop culture feel legalistic and forced or was it an opportunity to receive grace? Did your day of rest affect your reconnection with pop culture the rest of the week?

10. As ambassador parents, we're called to equip our kids for God's work in their generation and pray that they will be able to accomplish it. But we're not supposed to do this alone. Think of a few people in the circle around your family who invest in your kids. Offer a prayer of thanksgiving along the lines of David's as he received the help of the community to empower his son Solomon for the building of the temple:

> But who am I, and who are my people, that we should be able to give as generously as this? Everything comes from you, and we have given you only what comes from your hand. We are aliens and strangers in your sight, as were all our forefathers. Our days on earth are like a shadow, without hope. O LORD our God, as for all this abundance that we have provided for building you a temple for your Holy Name, it comes from your hand, and all of it belongs to you. I know, my God, that you test the heart and are pleased with integrity. All these things have I given willingly and with honest intent. And now I have seen with joy how willingly your people who are here have given to you. O LORD, God of our fathers Abraham, Isaac and Israel, keep this desire in the hearts of your people forever, and keep their hearts loyal to you. And give my son Solomon the wholehearted devotion to keep your commands, requirements and decrees and to do everything to build the palatial structure for which I have provided. (1 Chron. 29:14–19)

# 10

## Imagination

A diplomat tries to arouse the nation while a politician lulls it to sleep.

Anonymous

Tenacity is the dogged determination to stick it out despite hardships. But sometimes long-term public servants don't like to cause a stir. Journalist Nicholas Kraley interviewed dozens of U.S. foreign service officers to learn more about the day-to-day life of a diplomat. He described a bureaucratic inertia that hinders courage and creativity:

> A vast majority of the interviewed officers described the Foreign Service culture as risk-averse, and some said it lacks an "entrepreneurial spirit."
> "I have a phrase: pre-emptive capitulation," a senior officer in Latin America said. "There are a lot of officers who, if they know they are going to run into a problem, retreat from their

position. You shut your mouth because you know it's going to make trouble for your career."[1]

Effective ambassadors need more than just the ability to survive—they need a strong and free imagination to make an impact in the country of their posting. Employing that mature imagination, they take bold steps that bring about lasting change. Brazilian Sergio Vieira de Mello, a United Nations diplomat, was killed along with some twenty others in a 2003 truck-bomb attack in Baghdad. His eulogy in the *Christian Science Monitor* describes how a bold imagination made Vieira de Mello one of the best diplomats of our age:

> Despite the conservatism bred by the UN bureaucracy, [Vieira de Mello] maintained a willingness to take risks. In November 1999, armed with the broadest mandate to run a country in UN history, Vieira de Mello arrived in a smoldering East Timor. His job was to shepherd the tiny, barren half-island of 700,000 to a democratic birth after 500 years of Portuguese and Indonesian misrule. Within a day of arriving, he made the journey along a treacherous mountain road into the tiny nation's interior, where East Timor's independence hero and president-in-waiting, Xanana Gusmao, was holed up with his army.
>
> Aides warned against the trip, worried of conferring political legitimacy on any group before elections, and limiting the UN's scope to act. But Vieira de Mello immediately grasped that he needed local partners, not local suspicions, if his mission was to succeed.
>
> "We're not here to build a country," he told Mr. Gusmao, in the middle of a camp teeming with wild-haired guerrillas. "We're here to help you build a country." It was a moment typical of the political skills and audacity that made Vieira de Mello a legend at the organization.[2]

Like Vieira de Mello, diplomats for the King of Kings take risks that require creativity and courage. Ambassador families seek to move beyond the "culture wars"[3] that have distracted time and energy away from our calling to represent our King in every corner of the planet. To extend the influence of the kingdom, we need to nourish and free our own and our children's imaginations.

## Feed the Imagination

There are three sure ways to "grow" an imagination. The first is through *story*. If you asked me to evaluate myself as a parent, story is the one area where I'm confident of my success. There's no doubt in my mind that my children can affirm one stanza in Strickland Gillian's famous poem, "The Reading Mother":

You may have tangible wealth untold;
Caskets of jewels and coffers of gold.
Richer than I you can never be—
I had a Mother who read to me.[4]

Story was the one gift I could pass on that didn't require any special virtue or experience on my part. When it came to the awesome, scary job of parenting, storytelling was the one task where even a weak and silly creature couldn't go wrong.

I began reading aloud to our twins before they could toddle. I'd sit cross-legged on the bed, Indian-style, and prop them inside the crooks of my knees. Separating them with a pillow so they couldn't topple forward, I'd open a book on top of the pillow, and we'd read, read, and read some more. Through the years, the shared experience of story knit us together as a community, gave us points of reference for difficult conversations, and allowed the boys to explore intimate, passionate emotions without the intensity of a face-to-face interaction. As writer Ursula Le Guin put it, "a person who had never listened to nor read a tale or myth or parable or story would remain ignorant of his own emotional and spiritual heights and depths, [and] would not know quite fully what it is to be human."[5]

When our boys grew old enough to read for themselves, they still enjoyed hearing a story read aloud. On long drives, over dinner, in hotel rooms, beside the fire in our home, even sometimes as they gamed and listened simultaneously, we made our way through classics like the Chronicles of Narnia, *Grimm's Fairy Tales*, *The Hobbit*, the Lord of the Rings trilogy, *Little Men*, *The Five Little Peppers*, the Little House books, *Anne of Green Gables*, *Old Yeller*, *Understood Betsy*, *The Little Princess*, and *The Secret Garden*. We didn't care if they were "girl" books or "boy" books—we read them all. We consumed Bible stories and modern books (some via professional recordings), like Katherine Paterson's *The Same Stuff as Stars*, Judy Blume's Fudge books, the Harry Potter series, and any others that caught our fancy. We read books we loved, some we hated, and some that made us mad at the author but changed us forever. We cheered for heroes who overcame evil and raged over scenes where the weak were tormented and destroyed. We laughed and we cried. There was no need to censor as we read age-appropriate books together—we were together as we traveled far and wide and God was journeying with all of us.

Imagination is the ability to fill in the blanks deliberately woven into the story by the creator. As G. K. Chesterton pointed out, "Anybody who remembers a favorite fairy-story will have a strong sense of its original solidity and richness and even definite detail; and will be surprised, if he re-reads it in later life, to find how few and bald were the words which his own imagination made not only vivid but varied."[6]

We have to immerse our children in story to feed their imaginations so that they in turn can invent new stories. The great Christian artists of the past who made a profound impact

on culture consumed the works of others widely and voraciously. Ambassador families also must devour story, whether
pagan or Christian, classic or modern, on the page or on a
screen, academic or popular.

The second way to grow an imagination is through *play*.
When I visited the refugee camps along the Thai-Burma
border or the slum communities in India, I was struck by the
gleeful way children played. Using an old bicycle wheel and a
stick, for example, or a pile of pebbles, they invented countless
games and pastimes. When we returned to life in an American
suburb, I was shocked by the absence of play. Where *were* the
kids, anyway? David Elkind's *The Hurried Child* posited that
they were being shuttled from one adult-organized activity
to the next.[7] When they were at home, they didn't play—they
were entertained by other adult-generated activities. Kids in
Western cultures were forgetting how to play.

Play is defined as "activities bringing amusement or enjoyment, especially the spontaneous activity of young children
or young animals."[8] The intrinsic spontaneity of play is what
stimulates a young person's imagination. Without any adult
input, kids must come up with amusement or enjoyment. Be-
nign, distant parental vigilance steers them away from harmful
activities (to paraphrase G. K. Chesterton, when children are
bored, they tease the cat), but provides little or no direction.
Our children need an unhurried pace of life, freedom from
adult manipulation, and a fair amount of boredom to give
their imaginations scope for growth.

The third way to feed an imagination is through *stress*. As
parents, we often feel that our job description is to eliminate
any suffering from our children's lives. While we should protect, defend, and shield them with all our might from evil,
we cannot keep them from the painful results of the fall.
Weakness, rejection, failure, grief, betrayal—a parent's love is
unable to keep these and other kinds of suffering at bay. Nor

should we. Our call is to accompany our kids through such painful times, praying for them to receive the loving company, guidance, and healing of the King.

When my family moved from the diverse setting of Flushing, Queens, New York, to the white-bread world of suburban California, I entered the seventh grade as an unknown dark-skinned entity. Nobody talked to me for weeks. After a couple of months of desolation, I was standing alone in P.E. class as usual. The teacher appointed two of the most popular kids in the class to serve as captains. She disappeared somewhere to sneak a smoke while the two captains picked teams. Soon, there were only two of us left—a child with some kind of a mental disability and me.

One captain was a curly-haired, handsome kid who was renowned as the best athlete in the school. I can still see his face, although I don't remember his name. "Okay, okay," he groaned. "I'll take the black, ugly thing."

It took a full minute to realize he was talking about *me*. Even though I tried my best to exert self-control and not reveal the power he had to hurt me, the tears came anyway. But so did the comfort. Immediately, a circle of girls surrounded me like warrior queens. (In retrospect, I realize boys might have wanted to participate, but how could they at that socially awkward stage of life?) One girl rebuked the boy who had spoken. Others reached out to pat my back and shoulders. Still another thrust a tissue under the shield of hands I was using to hide my face.

I was never lonely in school again.

I didn't tell my parents about the rejection I experienced that day, but if they had known, what could they have done? They couldn't have closed that boy's mouth and kept his words from penetrating my soul. Nor, in retrospect, would I want them to. That formative moment of suffering and comfort informed my imagination about how it is to feel "other." Thanks to that experience of rejection and several others, I weave a heightened awareness of life on the margins into my writing and into my life.

Artists who become culture-shapers typically endure much more suffering as children than I did. C. S. Lewis and J. R. R. Tolkien, for example, both lost their mothers when they were young. As you read their works, you glimpse how the grief of their childhoods nourished their imaginations. In the same way, as our children suffer, they may grow in the ability to imagine what others might be enduring. As they receive comfort, they may become better able to imagine how to comfort others. Only an imagination saturated with empathy and mercy is able to weave culture on behalf of the King.

## Set the Imagination Free

We try to inform our children's imaginations so that they are equipped to discern the hidden agendas of the world's storytellers. But as ambassador families, we must go farther than that:

> Critical training, however, is but chipping at the top of the iceberg. It does not deal with the core of the problem facing Christian imaginations, namely, a failure to recognize and shoulder one's own unique vocation, to activate one's own creativity, for the sake of all.[9]

Why has the Christian imagination failed in this vocation during recent years? Primarily because it has been held captive within narrow confines.

Philip Pullman won the United Kingdom's prestigious 2002 Whitbread Book of the Year Prize for *The Amber Spyglass*, the last book in his Dark Materials trilogy. A reviewer described Pullman's view of Christianity:

[Pullman] gave a remarkable speech called "The Republic of Heaven" in which he succeeded in converting the words "God is dead" into something positive. He refreshingly recruited Jane Eyre to his cause while giving Tolkien and C. S. Lewis the thumbs down for failing to salute the real world. He is not short of faith but believes in humanity and in goodness, not in God.[10]

Surpassing Pullman's achievements, other artists have created new icons for Western culture. J. K. Rowling's Harry Potter series captured a generation of video gamers and turned them into avid readers. In George Lucas's Star Wars trilogy, Jedi heroes battle the dark side of the "Force." As a sign of their zealous commitment to the "Force," thousands of people in England, New Zealand, and Australia penciled in "Jedi" as their religion of choice.[11] The baton has passed from Tolkien and Lewis, who were unabashedly inside the church, to Pullman (an athiest or agnostic), Rowling (who rarely mentions God or church), and Lucas (who leans toward Buddhism) outside the church. We have to face the truth: followers of Jesus are not able to captivate and penetrate Western culture to the same extent as we used to.

When a work of literature captures the popular imagination, it expresses what C. G. Jung termed the "collective unconscious."[12] Jung believed that a devoted Christian would find it difficult to create fiction that rings true to this communal imagination. Closed systems of religion, he wrote, "have an undoubted tendency to suppress the unconscious in the individual as much as possible, thus paralyzing his fantasy activity."[13]

Over the past fifty years, the evangelical community has become increasingly a closed system, cloistered from the rest of culture. Instead of reflecting the questions and experiences within modern Western culture, the imaginations of evangelical artists today are paralyzed by life in the cloister. We create stories that provide answers instead of articulating the questions.

This was not the case for followers of Jesus who wrote before the 1960s. J. R. R. Tolkien, for example, was involved and enmeshed in wider British society. He was able to set his unconscious mind free to weave in the yearnings and questions of adolescence. Even today, readers respond to the Lord of the Rings trilogy because they recognize this work of fantasy as a "symbolic rendering(s) of (their) crucial life experiences," as psychologist Bruno Bettelheim put it.[14]

Can this trend be reversed? Can ambassadors of the kingdom once again shape and permeate the collective imagination? Only if our own imaginations are given free reign to guide the creative process. Nadine Gordimer, in her Nobel Prize acceptance speech, summed up the essence of life-changing art:

> This aesthetic venture of ours becomes subversive when the shameful secrets of our times are explored deeply, with the artist [maintaining a] rebellious integrity to the state of being manifest in life around her or him; then the writer's themes and characters inevitably are formed by the pressures and distortions of that society as the life of the fisherman is determined by the power of the sea.[15]

The safe, often rigid boundaries within the evangelical culture have governed and restricted the imagination, just as Jung predicted. If we closet our children away from popular culture, they'll have neither the freedom to create numinous stories, nor the grace to be informed by a boundlessly creative God. Trapped within such narrow confines, how can their imaginations reflect the "pressures and distortions" of the society around them?

Many artists recognize the presence of an outside muse actively involved in shaping their imaginations. The kingdom ambassador's imagination must be guided by the Holy Spirit, the Author of freedom, creativity, and life, not by any other muse—not even the set of limitations and regulations dictated by the evangelical subculture.

Todd Komarnicki (screenwriter and producer of the 2003 movie *Elf*) is one follower of Jesus who's trying to make a difference in Hollywood. Chris Monroe, staff writer for *Christian Spotlight on the Movies*, comments on the role of the Komarnicki parents in Todd's efforts:

> When Todd was just starting out in Los Angeles as a writer he always found that his parents were behind him. He says it would have been easy for them to wonder what he was doing, question whether or not he was being responsible, or think that it was "flighty" to chase his dream. But his parents were never like this. Instead, they encouraged him to follow his dream and to discover it as he goes. They exhorted him to stay focused on prayer and keep his head and heart where it should be. With the success that Todd has been experiencing as of late, it seems that this support has well paid off.[16]

Kristyn Komarnicki, Todd's sister, is the editor of Evangelicals for Social Action's *Prism* magazine. She speaks of the role her parents played traveling with them through the teen years and beyond:

> Our parents were the perfect combination of what Jesus calls for in Matthew 10:16: "Behold, I send you out as sheep in the midst of wolves; so be wise as serpents and innocent as doves." From our mother, I learned to be open, trusting, loving, giving as a dove. From our father, I learned to think, analyze, discern. This combination has served me well in my life of faith—I'm not afraid to reach out to others, not afraid of being engulfed by their needs or their different ways of life. Also, our parents gave us the FREEDOM TO FIND OUR OWN WAY, and the FREEDOM TO FAIL. This gave us the courage to try

almost anything, because you know you can always come home again afterwards! The prodigal son story says it all.[17]

Ambassador parents must provide opportunities to nourish and inform the imaginations of our children even as we set them free. Shattering Jung's gloomy predictions, followers of Jesus may once again weave in the deep questions of popular culture along with the eternal truths of his kingdom. Our kids may then weave enduring change into the world of popular culture:

> [Imagination] is the weaver of culture. . . . Educating the imagination—or controlling it—is thus of primordial importance. Advertisers, politicians, and totalitarian regimes have developed a science of this faculty, and a whole technology through which to manipulate it. Logically, Christians should be well armed against such manipulation. They are heirs to the greatest imaginative tradition alive on this planet. Adam is defined as created in the image of God. The Incarnation, the very heart of Salvation, is imaging: Paul preaches Christ as "the image of the invisible God" (Colossians 1:15). Being a Christian is being called to further imaging. That Divine Image must be transmitted in ever new contexts, in words, in stone, in paint, above all in flesh, our own flesh, in His body, the church. . . . The public still thirsts for the Beloved's face. . . . It is the Christian imagination's role to keep this thirst intense, by recalling that face, representing it over and over again.[18]

**Focus Story: Books**

Rosa was organizing the family room when she stumbled across the cheap paperback. *Love's True Kiss* was the title. On the cover, a buxom blonde leaned back into the muscular arms of a cowboy who gazed down at her adoringly. *Hmmm*, Rosa thought, turning the book over. "Beautiful socialite Tawny

173

Jones has always trusted God," she read, "but her heart's been broken by her childhood sweetheart. She leaves New England for her uncle's ranch and begins a summer of healing and romance. Read this exciting sequel to *Love's First Kiss* and discover how God works out all things for a girl who trusts in Him."

Rosa headed for the foot of the stairs. "Susana!" she called. "Venga aquí, mi amor."

"Yes, Mom?" Susana was thirteen, and as docile and loving of a daughter as Rosa and José could desire.

"Qué es este libro?" Rosa always reverted to Spanish when she was worried.

Susana blushed. "Oh, that. I found that in the church library."

"Mind if I read it, querida?"

"Ummm . . . no, Mom, go ahead. I actually haven't started it yet."

Rosa finished the book that night. The content confirmed her suspicions. Not only was this "Christian" book written to titillate young women, it overemphasized the thin, blond "beauty" of the main character and was replete with faulty prosperity theology. But what could Rosa do? She had never censored Susana's avid reading; she'd always encouraged it. In the world of pop culture, saturated with senseless violence and degradation, could a book like this really do any damage in her daughter's life?

### Put It into Practice

1. Should Rosa forbid her daughter to read this particular book? More generally, should parents ever censor a child's reading of literature? If so, when and how?
2. Some masterful authors invite us to enter and reside in a nihilistic world without hope or grace. (*The God of*

*Small Things* by Arundhati Roy, for example, despite or perhaps because of the author's lyrical, suspenseful prose, dampened one of our family vacations by depressing me thoroughly). Should we submit our imaginations to the "authority" of a writer whose worldview is fundamentally opposed to that of the Creator?

3. Peter Leithart suggests how a follower of Jesus should read fiction:

> Christian reading is not only about passing ethical judgments; it is also. . . about humbly and patiently learning the world that is the work. But Christian humility demands ethical-aesthetic judgments, because Christian humility is ultimately humility before God. Humility before God means agreeing with His judgments. No reader, of course, has a red phone to heaven, nor is there an inerrant and infallible Index of Forbidden Books. Yet God has passed judgment on certain things, and it would be remarkable arrogance for a Christian to disagree. We know that books are bad if they pattern our desires to hope for anonymous sex, if they encourage imitation of characters who scorn God, if they invite us to see the world as a cosmic toilet.
>
> Once ethical criteria are brought into play, the question of whether a book should be read at all must be addressed. Frenzied cries of censorship should not deter anyone from pursuing the question. Given the important role that humility plays in reading, one key set of questions to ask is, "Do I wish to submit to this author? Is the pattern of desire that this book encourages healthy or unhealthy? Does the writer present models that may be imitated, or negative models as warnings? Will my involvement with the world and its Creator be enriched by seeing the world as the author wishes me to see it? Will my learning my way around his fictional world improve me or set me back?"[19]

175

Consider the last novel you read and answer Leithart's questions about it. Are you glad you completed the book?

4. The feeding of the imagination is perhaps as important as the diet of top athletes (cotton candy is permissible but not beneficial eaten as breakfast on a regular basis). Name three books or magazines you've read recently. Are they more like candy for the soul or like whole-grain bread? Have you been nourishing your imagination with a balanced diet?

## Bringing It Home (for the Family or Small Group)

5. When was the last time you were bored and what did you do about it? Parents: How did you play as a kid? Kids: Describe a spontaneous enjoyable activity that you initiated recently (no adult involvement allowed).

6. Share one or two experiences of suffering in your childhood that shaped your ability to empathize or offer comfort.

7. C. S. Lewis believed in reading a book more than once:

> The sure mark of the unliterary man is that he considers "I've read it already" to be a conclusive argument against reading a work. . . . Those who read great works, on the other hand, will read the same work ten, twenty or thirty times during the course of their life.[20]

Have you ever reread a novel? If so, which one? Why do you think you revisited that particular story?

8. Try to articulate a group or family definition of a "Christian" book (i.e., the author mentioned the name of Jesus or it was written by a follower of Jesus, etc.). Get started by reading the opinions of two authors whose books have won the Newbery Prize, the American Library Association's top award given to books for young readers:

176

Katherine Paterson [author of *Bridge to Terabithia*]: The challenge for those of us who care about our faith and about a hurting world is to tell stories which will carry the words of grace and hope in their bones and sinews and not wear them like fancy dress.[21]

Madeleine L'Engle [author of *A Wrinkle in Time*]: The journey homewards. Coming home. That's what it's all about. The journey to the coming of the Kingdom. That's probably the chief difference between the Christian and the secular artist—the purpose of the work, be it story or music or painting, is to further the coming of the kingdom, to make us aware of our status as children of God, and to turn our feet toward home.[22]

# Conclusion

Rob and I were studying Hindi in the Himalayan foothills when we met David. He seemed as young and broke and scruffy as we were, and the three of us hit it off.

"Come to Delhi and visit," he urged. "My parents would love to meet you." He scribbled an address before heading down to the plains.

Once our language intensive was over, we decided to accept his invitation. We endured the dusty bus journey and disembarked in the crowded, narrow streets of Old Delhi. Hailing a battered rickshaw-taxi, we gave the driver the address that David had written down. The driver's eyebrows lifted but he didn't say anything.

As we careened closer to our destination, we began to notice the streets becoming wider and cleaner. Houses were set away from the road behind high gates and we glimpsed gardens and marble and fountains. The rickshaw-taxi dropped us off in front of the most ornate gate of all. On either side, proud red and white flags with maple leaves billowed in the afternoon breeze. The guard asked us doubtfully whom we wanted, taking stock of our graduate student attire, which included the standard well-traveled backpack and athletic shoes.

"We're here to see David," we answered.

The guard phoned up to the house and the gates swung wide. We walked slowly up the long, curving driveway, lined with magnolia trees and bougainvillea. The door flew open and there was David. "I'm so glad you're here," he said. "Come meet my parents."

David's mother was a gracious woman who immediately took us under her wing. "Stay for dinner," she insisted. "We'd love to have you."

We'd known that David's dad worked for the Canadian government but we hadn't realized that he was *the* High Commissioner—the equivalent of an ambassador, the highest ranking foreign officer representing Canada. The dinner guests that night included Chuck Colson, who was visiting India's prisons on behalf of Prison Fellowship, several Indian and Canadian dignitaries, and two young American graduate students (us). We feasted at a table resplendent with silver, china, and crystal, remembering vaguely that our last meal had been a two-rupee samosa bought from a roadside stand.

Every time we passed through Delhi, David's mom insisted that we stay with them even when David wasn't there. Fluffy white linens, full breakfasts served in a serene back garden with parrots flitting from tree to tree, tennis on impeccable clay courts at the Canadian Club ... we didn't protest too much. Always, she and the High Commissioner welcomed us with genuine pleasure, spending as much time with us as they could. Rested and refreshed, we left their home convinced that if *these* were the people Canadians had chosen to represent their country, it must be a wonderful place indeed. To this day, we love Canada and seize any chance we get to visit—possibly because it brings back delightful memories of our first introduction to that country.

I often recall David and his family when I reflect on our role as family ambassadors. Do we welcome strangers, even unlikely, bedraggled foreigners, to our feast as warmly as David's parents did to theirs? Are host-country residents intrigued enough by our interactions to learn more about our native land? Or better still, to meet our King?

In my travels far and wide, I've encountered a group of people who grew up straddling borders. They're sometimes called "Third Culture Kids"—children of ambassadors, missionaries, and businesspeople who are raised in other countries but retain their citizenship in their parents' home countries. There are losses associated with life as a Third Culture Kid, mostly because they feel as if they don't fit in anywhere. But the gains of life along the border are abundant. Third Culture Kids realize early that virtues are not the property of one culture or generation. They recognize the ache that makes everybody feel like strangers, even in the middle of comfortable homogeneity. That's what makes them exponentially better than the average person at crossing borders.

In a sense, ambassador families as described in this book are raising Third Culture Kids. If our children accept the vocation of diplomacy, they may not fit neatly into the subcultures of our churches. A touch of cultural schizophrenia comes with the territory of the diplomatic lifestyle. Hopefully, our kids won't feel at home in Samaria either, because they delight in their heavenly citizenship.

The Gospel writers describe how Jesus interacted with Samaria—he crossed borders, faced hostility, sought the familiar, pursued the outsider, and spoke the language. He wasn't daunted in his travels, even when judged by his own people. As Jesus' ambassadors in the foreign world of popular culture, we strive to nurture our own and our kids' patriotism, *savoir-faire*, tenacity, and imagination. The end result, if all goes well, is a revolutionary transformation of that host country and her residents on behalf of our King.

# Appendix

## Resources for the Ambassador Family

Warning: Read or visit any of these resources at your own risk. Inclusion of a book or Web site does not necessarily imply endorsement of content. Please note also that this is not an exhaustive list, but provides a starting place for further research and reflection. Items are not listed in order of priority or excellence. For updated resources and links, or to add to this list, visit http://www.ambassadorfamilies.com/.

### Books on Faith and Culture

Rodney Clapp, *Border Crossings: Christian Trespasses on Popular Culture and Public Affairs* (Grand Rapids: Brazos, 2000).
————, *A Peculiar People: The Church as Culture in a Post-Christian Society* (Downers Grove, IL: InterVarsity, 1996).
David Dark, *Everyday Apocalypse: The Sacred Revealed in Radiohead, the Simpsons, and Other Pop Culture Icons* (Grand Rapids: Brazos, 2002).

William A. Dyrness, *The Earth Is God's: A Theology of American Culture* (Maryknoll, NY: Orbis, 1997).

John Fischer, *Fearless Faith: Living beyond the Walls of "Safe" Christianity* (Eugene, OR: Harvest House, 2002).

Os Guinness, *Fit Bodies, Fat Minds: Why Evangelicals Don't Think and What to Do about It* (Grand Rapids: Baker, 1994).

Stanley Hauerwas and William H. Willimon, *Resident Aliens: Life in the Christian Colony* (Nashville: Abingdon, 1989).

David W. Henderson, *Culture Shift: Communicating God's Truth to Our Changing World* (Grand Rapids: Baker, 1998).

Dick Keyes, *True Heroism in a World of Celebrity Counterfeits* (Colorado Springs: NavPress, 1999).

Gordon Lynch, *Understanding Theology and Popular Culture* (Malden, MA: Blackwell, 2005).

Brian D. McLaren and Tony Campolo, *Adventures in Missing the Point: How the Culture-Controlled Church Neutered the Gospel* (Grand Rapids: Zondervan, 2003).

Richard J. Mouw, *Consulting the Faithful: What Christian Intellectuals Can Learn from Popular Religion* (Grand Rapids: Eerdmans, 1994).

————, *He Shines in All That's Fair: Culture and Common Grace* (Grand Rapids: Eerdmans, 2002).

Kenneth Myers, *All God's Children and Blue Suede Shoes: Christians and Popular Culture* (Wheaton, IL: Crossway, 1989).

Lesslie Newbigin, *Truth and Authority in Modernity*, (Harrisburg, PA: Morehouse, 1996).

H. Richard Niebuhr, *Christ and Culture* (San Francisco: HarperSanFrancisco, 1956).

James I. Packer, *God Has Spoken* (Downers Grove, IL: InterVarsity, 1979).

William D. Romanowski, *Eyes Wide Open: Looking for God in Popular Culture* (Grand Rapids: Brazos, 2001).

————, *Pop Culture Wars: Religion and the Role of Entertainment in American Life* (Downers Grove, IL: InterVarsity, 1996).

Dick Staub, *Too Christian—Too Pagan: How to Love the World without Falling for It* (Grand Rapids: Zondervan, 2000).

John R. W. Stott, *Involvement: Vol. 1, Being a Responsible Christian in a Non-Christian Society* (Grand Rapids: Revell, 1984).

## Books on Faith and Art

Hilary Brand and Adrienne Chaplin, *Art and Soul: Signposts for Christians in the Arts* (Downers Grove, IL: InterVarsity, 2001).

Michael Card, *Scribbling in the Sand: Christ and Creativity* (Downers Grove, IL: InterVarsity, 2002).

Andrew M. Greeley, *The Catholic Imagination* (Berkeley: University of California Press, 2000).

Os Guinness, *Prophetic Untimeliness: A Challenge to the Idol of Relevance* (Grand Rapids: Baker, 2003).

Leland Ryken, ed., *The Christian Imagination* (New York: Waterbrook, 2002).

Steve Turner, *Imagine: A Vision for Christians in the Arts* (Downers Grove, IL: InterVarsity, 2001).

## Books on General Media

Gil Bailie, *Violence Unveiled: Humanity at the Crossroads* (New York: Crossroad, 1997).

Dave Grossman, *Stop Teaching Our Kids to Kill: A Call to Action Against TV, Movie, and Video Game Violence* (New York: Crown, 1999).

W. James Potter, *The 11 Myths of Media Violence* (Thousand Oaks, CA: Sage, 2002).

Quentin J. Schultze, *Communicating for Life: Christian Stewardship in Community and Media* (Grand Rapids: Baker Academic, 2000).

Victor C. Strasburger and Barbara J. Wilson, *Children, Adolescents, and the Media* (Thousand Oaks, CA: Sage, 2002).

Richard Winter, *Still Bored in a Culture of Entertainment: Rediscovering Passion and Wonder* (Downers Grove, IL: InterVarsity, 2002).

## Books on Movies

Philip Longfellow Anderson, Franklin Thomas, and Ollie Johnston, *The Gospel according to Disney: Christian Values in the Early Animated Classics* (La Canada, CA: Longfellow, 1999).

Ken Gire, *Reflections on the Movies: Hearing God in the Unlikeliest of Places* (Colorado Springs: Chariot Victor, 2000).

Brian Godawa, *Hollywood Worldviews: Watching Films with Wisdom and Discernment* (Downers Grove, IL: InterVarsity, 2002).

Gareth Higgins, *How Movies Helped Save My Soul: Finding Spiritual Fingerprints in Culturally Significant Films* (Lake Mary, FL: Relevant, 2003).

Robert K. Johnston, *Reel Spirituality: Theology and Film in Dialogue* (Grand Rapids: Baker Academic, 2000).

John Shelton Lawrence and Robert Jewett, *The Myth of the American Superhero* (Grand Rapids: Eerdmans, 2002).

Edward McNulty, *Praying the Movies: Daily Meditations from Classic Films* (Louisville: Geneva Press, 2001).

————, *Praying the Movies II: More Daily Meditations from Classic Films* (Louisville: Westminster John Knox, 2004).

Bryan P. Stone, *Faith and Film: Theological Themes at the Cinema* (St. Louis: Chalice, 2000).

## Books on Television

Walter T. Davis, Jr., Gary Dreibelbis, and Teresa Blythe, *Watching What We Watch: Prime-Time Television through the Lens of Faith* (Louisville: Westminster John Knox, 2001).

Philip D. Patterson, *Stay Tuned: What Every Parent Should Know about Media* (Webb City, MO: Covenant, 2002).

Mark I. Pinsky, *The Gospel according to The Simpsons: The Spiritual Life of the World's Most Animated Family* (Louisville: Westminster John Knox, 2001).

Quentin J. Schultze, *Redeeming Television* (Downers Grove, IL: InterVarsity, 1992).

Debra Koontz Traverso, *TV Time: 150 Fun Family Activities That Turn Your Television into a Learning Tool* (New York: Avon, 1998).

## Books on the Internet

Andrew Careaga, *Hooked on the Net: How to Say "Goodnight" When the Party Never Ends* (Grand Rapids: Kregel, 2002).

Douglas Groothuis, *The Soul in Cyberspace* (Grand Rapids: Baker, 1997).

Quentin J. Schultze, *Habits of the High-Tech Heart: Living Virtuously in the Information Age* (Grand Rapids: Baker Academic, 2002).

————, *Internet for Christians: Everything You Need to Start Cruising the Net Today* (Muskegon, MI: Gospel Films, 1998).

Donald Tapscott, *Growing Up Digital: The Rise of the Net Generation* (New York: McGraw-Hill, 1998).

## Books on Music

Peter Christenson and Donald Roberts, *It's Not Only Rock and Roll: Popular Music in the Lives of Adolescents* (Cresskill, NJ: Hampton, 1998).

Andy Greenwald, *Nothing Feels Good: Punk Rock, Teenagers, and Emo* (New York: St. Martin's, 2003).

Mark Joseph, *Faith, God, and Rock + Roll: From Bono to Jars of Clay: How People of Faith Are Transforming American Popular Music* (Grand Rapids: Baker, 2003).

————, *The Rock & Roll Rebellion: Why People of Faith Abandoned Rock Music and Why They're Coming Back* (Nashville: Broadman & Holman, 1999).

Charlie Peacock, *At the Crossroads: An Insider's Look at the Past, Present, and Future of Contemporary Christian Music* (Nashville: Broadman & Holman, 1999).

Quentin J. Schultze and Roy M. Anker, *Dancing in the Dark* (Grand Rapids: Eerdmans, 1991).

John J. Thompson and Dinah K. Kotthoff, *Raised by Wolves: The Story of Christian Rock & Roll* (Toronto: ECW, 2000).

Steve Turner, *Hungry for Heaven: Rock 'n' Roll and the Search for Redemption* (Downers Grove, IL: InterVarsity, 1995).

Alonzo Westbrook, *Hip Hoptionary: The Dictionary of Hip Hop Terminology* (New York: Harlem Moon/Broadway Books, 2002).

## Books on Reading

Bruno Bettelheim, *The Uses of Enchantment: The Meaning and Importance of Fairy Tales* (New York: Vintage, 1989).

Matthew T. Dickerson, *Following Gandalf: Epic Battles and Moral Victory in the Lord of the Rings* (Grand Rapids: Brazos, 2003).

Mem Fox, *Reading Magic: Why Reading Aloud to Our Children Will Change Their Lives Forever* (Eugene, OR: Harvest, 2001).

James W. Kemp, *The Gospel According to Dr. Seuss: Snitches, Sneetches, and Other "Creachas"* (Valley Forge, PA: Judson, 2004).

C. S. Lewis, *An Experiment in Criticism* (Cambridge, UK: Cambridge University Press, 1992).

Connie Neal, *The Gospel According to Harry Potter: Spirituality in the Stories of the World's Most Famous Seeker* (Louisville: Westminster John Knox, 2002).

Jim Trelease, *The Read-Aloud Handbook,* 5th ed. (New York: Penguin, 2001).

## Books on General Parenting

Stephen Arterburn and Fred Stoeker, *Preparing Your Son for Every Man's Battle* (New York: Waterbrook, 2003).

George Barna, *Transforming Children into Spiritual Champions* (Ventura, CA: Gospel Light, 1999).

Bill Beausay, *Teenage Boys! Surviving and Enjoying These Extraordinary Years* (New York: Waterbrook, 2001).

Gary D. Chapman and Ross Campbell, *The Five Love Languages of Children* (Chicago: Moody, 1997).

Henry Cloud and John Townsend, *Boundaries with Kids* (Grand Rapids: Zondervan, 2001).

Marva Dawn, *Is It a Lost Cause? Having the Heart of God for the Church's Children* (Grand Rapids: Eerdmans, 1997).

James C. Dobson, *Bringing Up Boys: Practical Advice and Encouragement for Those Shaping the Next Generation of Men* (Carol Stream, IL: Tyndale, 2001).

———, *The New Dare to Discipline* (Carol Stream, IL: Tyndale, 1996).

———, *The New Strong-Willed Child: Birth through Adolescence* (Carol Stream, IL: Tyndale, 2004).

———, *Parenting Isn't for Cowards* (Nashville: Nelson, 1993).

———, *Preparing for Adolescence: How to Survive the Coming Years of Change* (Ventura, CA: Regal, 1999).

Karen Dockrey, *Bold Parents, Positive Teens* (New York: Waterbrook, 2002).

Sharon A. Hersh *Mom, I Feel Fat: Becoming Your Daughter's Ally in Developing a Healthy Body Image* (New York: Waterbrook, 2001).

Kevin Huggins, *Parenting Adolescents* (Colorado Springs: NavPress, 1989).

Margaret J. Meeker, *Restoring the Teenage Soul: Nurturing Sound Hearts and Minds in a Confused Culture* (Traverse City, MI: McKinley & Mann, 1999).

Walt Mueller, *Understanding Today's Youth Culture* (Carol Stream, IL: Tyndale, 1999).

Connie Neal, *Walking Tall in Babylon: Raising Children to Be Godly and Wise in a Perilous World* (New York: Waterbrook, 2003).

Stormie Omartian, *The Power of a Praying Parent* (Eugene, OR: Harvest House, 1995).

Eugene H. Peterson, *Like Dew Your Youth: Growing Up with Your Teenager* (Grand Rapids: Eerdmans, 1998).

Dennis and Barbara Rainey, *Parenting Today's Adolescent* (Nashville: Nelson, 2002).

David John Seel, Jr., *Parenting without Perfection: Being a Kingdom Influence in a Toxic World* (Colorado Springs: NavPress, 2000).

Tim Stafford, *Never Mind the Joneses* (Downers Grove, IL: InterVarsity, 2004).

Jim and Janet Sundberg, *How to Win at Sports Parenting: Maximizing the Sports Experience for You and Your Child* (New York: Waterbrook, 2000).

Paul David Tripp, *Age of Opportunity: A Biblical Guide to Parenting Teens* (Phillipsburg, NJ: P & R, 1997).

## Books on Parenting in Crisis Situations

Melody Carlson, Heather Kopp, and Linda Clare, *Lost Boys and the Moms Who Love Them* (New York: Waterbrook, 2002).

Scott Larson, *When Teens Stray: Parenting for the Long Haul* (Ventura, CA: Vine, 2002).

Scott Larson and Larry Brendtro, *Reclaiming Our Prodigal Sons and Daughters: A Practical Approach for Connecting with Youth in Conflict* (Bloomington, IN: National Educational Service, 2000).

Buddy Scott, *Relief for Hurting Parents: How to Fight for the Lives of Teenagers* (Lake Jackson, TX: Allon, 1989).

Rosalind Wiseman, *Queen Bees and Wannabees: Helping Your Daughter Survive Cliques, Gossip, Boyfriends, and Other Realities of Adolescence* (New York: Three Rivers, 2003).

## Books on Parenting and Consumer Culture

Rodney Clapp, ed., *The Consuming Passion: Christianity and the Consumer Culture* (Downers Grove, IL: InterVarsity, 1998).

David Elkind, *The Hurried Child: Growing Up Too Fast Too Soon*, 3d ed. (Cambridge, MA: Perseus, 2001).

Jan Johnson, *Growing Compassionate Kids: Helping Kids See beyond Their Backyard* (Nashville: Upper Room, 2001).

Neil Postman, *Amusing Ourselves to Death: Public Discourse in the Age of Show Business* (New York: Penguin, 1986).

———, *The Disappearance of Childhood* (New York: Vintage, 1994).

Tom Sine, *Mustard Seed versus McWorld: Reinventing Life and Faith for the Future* (Grand Rapids: Baker, 1999).

Anne Sutherland and Beth Thompson, *Kidfluence: The Marketer's Guide to Understanding and Reaching Generation Y-Kids, Tweens, and Teens* (New York: McGraw-Hill, 2003).

## Links on General Pop Culture

http://www.adbusters.org/home/index.html
   Adbusters: Culture Jammer Headquarters
http://www.americanpopularculture.com/
   The American Popular Culture Online Magazine
http://www.imagesjournal.com/
   Images: A Journal of Film and Popular Culture
http://www.kff.org/
   The Henry J. Kaiser Family Foundation: A Nonprofit Private Operating Foundation Focusing on the Major Health Care Issues Facing the Nation

http://popmatters.com/
   pop matters: the magazine of global culture
http://www.wsu.edu/%7Eamerstu/pop/tvrguide.html
   Popular Culture: Links and Resources for Critical
   Analysis


## Links on Pop Culture and Faith

http://www.christianitytoday.com/books/
   Books and Culture: A Christian Review
http://www.pfm.org/BPTemplate.cfm
   Breakpoint: To develop and communicate Christian worldview messages that offer a critique of contemporary culture and encourage and equip the church to think and live
   Christianly
http://www.youmagazine.com/
   Catholic Youth Online
http://www.crisismagazine.com/
   Crisis: Politics, Culture, and the Church
http://www.marshillforum.org/
   Mars Hill: Essays, Studies, Reminders of God
http://www.mckenziestudycenter.org/
   McKenzie Study Center: A ministry devoted to the study
   of the Bible and the promotion of a Christian worldview
http://www.neoscosmos.com/
   Neo's Cosmos: A Generation in Motion
http://www.ransomfellowship.org/
   Ransom Fellowship: Developing Discernment, Deepening
   Discipleship
http://www.dickstaub.com/
   Dick Staub: Where Belief Meets Real Life

## Links on General Media

http://www.savingchildhood.org/
   Bruderhof Saving Childhood Forum: For anyone who believes children need and deserve time and space simply to be children, free from the pressures and influences that await them in our success-driven, image-conscious, materialistic, technological age
http://www.medialit.org/
   Center for Media Literacy: Empowerment Through Education
http://www.futureofchildren.org/index.htm/
   The Future of Children: A Publication of Princeton-Brookings: Providing Research and Analysis to Promote Effective Policies and Programs for Children
http://www.lionlamb.org/
   The Lion and Lamb Project: Violence Is Not Child's Play
http://www.ministryandmedia.com/
   Ministry and Media: Reviews and Discussion Starters for Youth Workers
http://www.truelies.org/index.htm
   True Lies: Who Has Your Students' Attention and What Is Their Message?


## Links on Movies

http://www.pluggedinonline.com
   Focus on the Family
http://www.christianitytoday.com/movies
   Christianity Today: Movies

http://christiananswers.net/spotlight/home.html/

Christian Spotlight on Entertainment (includes e-games)

http://www.cleanfilms.com/

Clean Films: Rent and Buy Family Edited DVD Movies

http://www.dove.org/

Dove Family Approved Videos, Movies, and Video Games

http://www.faithnfilm.com/

Faith and Film: Daily News Coverage of Faith and Film

http://www.familystyle.com/

FamilyStyle Film Guide: Movie Reviews For Parents

http://www.gradingthemovies.com/

Grading the Movies, Music, and Games: Helping Families Find Entertainment with Values

http://www.hollywoodjesus.com/

Hollywood Jesus: Pop Culture from a Spiritual Point of View

http://www.nytimes.com/learning/parents/movieguide/

The New York Times Family Movie Guide

http://www.screenit.com/

Screen It: Entertainment Reviews for Parents

http://www.nccbuscc.org/movies/

U.S. Conference of Catholic Bishops Movie Reviews

## Links on Television

http://www.mediafamily.org/facts/facts_vlent.shtml/

National Institute on Media and the Family: Get Media-*Wise*/Watch what your kids watch.

http://www.parentstv.org

Parents' Television Council: Because Our Children Are Watching

http://www.tvturnoff.org/index.htm/

TV Turnoff Network: Help Kids Love Reading

## Links on Music

http://www.christianitytoday.com/music/

Christianity Today: Music

http://www.almenconi.com/

Al Menconi Ministries: Helping Parents Communicate Values to Their Children

## Links on General Parenting

http://www.cpyu.org/

Center for Parent Youth Understanding: Understanding Today's Youth Culture

http://cci.gospelcom.net/ccihome/

Christian Camping International, USA: Online Directory of 1000-plus member organizations, most of which offer a variety of accommodations, activities, and services for your children, family, or group (some provide scholarships)

http://www.christianitytoday.com/parenting/

Christian Parenting: Building Faith-Filled Families

http://www.homefaith.com/

The Claretians: Spiritual Help for Families

http://www.family.org/

Focus on the Family: To cooperate with the Holy Spirit in disseminating the gospel of Jesus Christ to as many people as possible, and, specifically, to accomplish that objective by helping to preserve traditional values and the institution of the family

http://www.healthyfamiliesnow.org
  Healthy Families Now: Helping Families Enrich Their
  Spiritual and Physical Health
http://www.media-awareness.ca/english/parents/index.cfm
  Media Awareness Network: Practical Tips for Helping Par-
  ents Manage Media in the Home
http://www.osv.com/periodicals/periodicals.asp?id=19
  Our Sunday Visitor: Catholic Parent
http://www.ipj-ppj.org/families.htm
  Parenting for Peace and Justice Network: Resources

# Notes

## Introduction

1. William Romanowski defines pop culture as "the network or system of shared meaning in a society, a conceptual collection of ideals, beliefs and values, ideas and knowledge, attitudes and assumptions about life that is woven together over time and is widely shared among a people.... [It] also describes the 'texts' of everyday life and material works that are a manifestation of [that]cultural system. *Pop Culture Wars: Religion and the Role of Entertainment in American Life* (Downers Grove, IL: InterVarsity, 1996), 306.

2. Dirck Halstead, "White Christmas," *Digital Journalist*, http://www.digital journalist.org/issue0005/ch9.htm.

3. Graham Martin, "On the 10th Anniversary of the Fall of Saigon," *New York Times*, April 30, 1985.

4. Nicholas Kraler, "Life as a Diplomat," Special Report, "America's Other Army: Inside the Foreign Service," *Washington Times*, April 19, 2004. Also available online at http://www.nicholaskraler.com/WT-FS-8.html.

5. Nicholas Kraler, "Consular Affairs," Special Report, "America's Other Army: Inside the Foreign Service," *Washington Times*, March 29, 2004. Also available online at http://www.nicholaskraler.com/WT-FS-5.html.

6. "Communication Problems," troubledwith.com, a ministry of Focus on the Family, http://www.troubledwith.com/Web/groups/public/@fotf_troubledwith/documents/articles/twi_topic_008626.cfm.

## Chapter 1: Following Jesus into Uncharted Territory

1. Inaugural Address, January 20, 1961, "Public Papers of the Presidents of the United States: John F. Kennedy, 1961"

2. ABC News Online, http://abcnews.go.com/sections/GMA/Entertain ment/GMA030820Thirteen_feature.html.

3. *Aladdin*, Disney, November 1992.

4. Dick Staub, *Staubthoughts: Bridging Faith and Culture*, http://www.dickstaub .com, CRS Communications, August 27, 2002.

5. Denis Haack, "Christian Discernment 101," http://www.ransom fellowship .org/D_101.html#questions. Used by permission.

6. Brother Lawrence, *The Practice of the Presence of God* (Grand Rapids: Revell/ Spire, 1967).

## Chapter 2: Following Jesus into Hostile Places

1. Speech to the House of Commons, February 28, 1991.

2. Focus on the Family has clarified that statement on their Web site. See "Dr. Dobson's (Comparatively) Liberal Views on Public Education," Marc Fey and Focus on the Family Research Team, December 2003, http://www.family. org/cforum/fosi/education/pe/a0026660.cfm.

3. American Psychiatric Association, "Teen Suicide," http://www.psych.org/ public_info/teen.cfm.

4. Donna Engelgau, "Cutting: The New-Age Anorexia," Discovery Health Channel, http://health.discovery.com/premiers/cutters/articles/goodstein_qa/good stein_qa.html.

5. Parents' Television Council analysts reviewed the video games advertised on programs airing during the November 2001 and May 2002 network sweeps periods. During the family hour (8–9 p.m.), a full 30 percent of all the video games advertised were rated M. On programs outside the family hour, but with more than 20 percent of the audience under 18, 40 percent of the video games advertised were assigned an M rating. All of the M-rated video games advertised during the study period appeared on Fox, WB, and UPN. The WB led the pack with M-rated video games making up 42 percent of its video-game commercials. ABC, CBS, and NBC only advertised video games rated E. Parents' Television Council press release, http:// www.parentstv.org/PTC/publications/release/2002/pr062802.asp.

6. Parents' Television Council review, http://www.parentstv.org/ptc/videogames/ reviews/vicecity.asp.

7. Sara Gaines, "Why Sex Still Leads the Net," *Guardian Unlimited*, February 28, 2002. Also online at http://www.guardian.co.uk/Archive/Article/0,4273,4364626,00 .html.

8. "Child abuse, child pornography and the internet," NCH: the children's char- ity, January 2004.

9. Kelly Sobczak, BootsnAll.com, http://www.bootsnall.com/travelstories/ me/nov01anger1.shtml.

10. Testimony before the Senate Foreign Relations Committee, Washington, DC, October 28, 2003.

11. "Recent Victories," The Rutherford Institute, http://www.rutherford.org/about/recent_victories.asp.

12. "The Rutherford Institute Legal Update," May 3, 2004, http://www.rutherford.org/articles_db/legal_features.asp?article_id=78.

## Chapter 3: Following Jesus to Hunt for Treasure

1. "Cecile, ou L'ecole des pères (Cecile, or the School for Fathers) (Comédie des Champs-Elysées, 1959).

2. Kimberley Locke, *One Love*, compact disc, Stiletto Entertainment, 2004, Curb Records D2-78845.

3. Craig A. Anderson, Nicholas L. Carnagey, and Janie Eubanks, "Exposure to Violent Media: The Effects of Songs with Violent Lyrics on Aggressive Thoughts and Feelings," *Journal of Personality and Social Psychology* 84 (5): 960–71.

4. Plato, *Republic*, book 4.

5. Ralph Graves, "An Infinity of Jimis: Rock Musician Jimi Hendrix in His Own Words and Some Appropriately Bizarre Pictures," *Life* 67 (14): 74.

6. Jesus replied: "'Love the Lord your God with all your heart and with all your soul and with all your mind.' This is the first and greatest commandment. And the second is like it: 'Love your neighbor as yourself.' All the Law and the Prophets hang on these two commandments" (Matt. 22:37–40).

7. Andrew Greeley, *God in Popular Culture* (Chicago: Thomas More, 1998).

8. Richard Mouw, *He Shines in All That's Fair: Culture and Common Grace* (Grand Rapids: Eerdmans, 2003).

9. Reformed Church theologian Abraham Kuyper believed that God's saving grace in Jesus Christ (*genade* in Dutch) was only for the elect. Besides God's special grace for the elect, though, Kuyper taught that God has a common grace for all people (*gratie* in Dutch). Kuyper develops this doctrine in his three-volume work, *De Gemeene Gratie* (On Common Grace), published in 1902–1904. Excerpts from this work translated into English may be found in *Abraham Kuyper: A Centennial Reader*, edited by James D. Bratt (Grand Rapids: Eerdmans, 1998).

10. David Neff, "The Uncommon Benefits of Common Grace," interview with Richard Mouw, *Christianity Today* 46 (8): 50.

11. Os Guinness, *Fit Bodies, Fat Minds: Why Evangelicals Don't Think and What to Do About It* (Grand Rapids: Baker, 1994), 132.

12. John R. W. Stott, *Involvement*. Vol. 1, *Being a Responsible Christian in a Non-Christian Society* (Grand Rapids: Revell, 1984), 56.

13. James I. Packer, *God Has Spoken* (Downers Grove, IL: InterVarsity, 1979), 8–9.

14. "The Christian Rocker's Creed," *CCM Magazine*, November 1988, 12.

15. Aristotle, *Republic*, Politics, 8, 1340, quoted in Donald J. Grout, *A History of Western Music* (New York: Norton, 1980), 8.

16. Said by Darko Velichkovski in "Church Debates Relevancy, Message of Contemporary Christian Music," www.lifeway.com, LifeWay Christian Resources, 2001–2003.

17. Martin Luther, quoted in Friedrich Blume, *Protestant Church Music* (New York: Norton, 1974), 10.

## Chapter 4: Following Jesus to Find the Outsider

1. Evan Esar, ed., *Dictionary of Humorous Quotations* (Mattituck, NY: Amereon, Ltd., 1976).

2. Novelist Emmi Fredericks coined the word "celebraholism" to describe "a complex psychological disorder characterized by an excessive, compulsive need for exposure to celebrities." *Fatal Distraction* (New York: Thomas Dunne Books, 2004), 1.

3. Karen Armstrong, "From Buddha to Beckham," *The Guardian*, June 12, 2004.

4. Dick Keyes, *True Heroism in a World of Celebrity Counterfeits* (Colorado Springs, CO: NavPress, 1999).

## Chapter 5: Following Jesus to Speak the Language

1. William Safire, *Words of Wisdom* (New York: Simon and Schuster/Fireside, 1989), 49.

2. "Diplomatic Readiness: The Human Strategy" (Washington, DC: U.S. Department of State, 2002), 23.

3. Matthew Arnold, "The Buried Life," lines 45–54, in Leider, Lovett, and Root, eds., *British Poetry and Prose*, vol. 2, 3d ed. (Boston: Houghton Mifflin, 1950).

4. Michael Card, "The Deep Desire to Be Known," *Teens 4 Jesus*, March 4, 2004. See http://t4jmag.com/past_issues/2004/mar04/cardstudy.shtm.

5. Francis de Laboulaye, "Qualifications of an Ambassador," selected essays, http://www.ediplomat.com.

## Chapter 6: Following Jesus When Others Judge You

1. William Ury, *Getting Past No: Negotiating Your Way from Confrontation to Cooperation* (New York: Bantam, 1993), 3.

2. Catherine Donaldson-Evans, "Jesus Chic Is Latest Fashion Trend," http://www.foxnews.com, May 10, 2004.

3. Dannah Gresh, "The Fashion Battle: Is It One Worth Fighting?" http://cbn.org/spirituallife/discipleship/gresh_fashion1102.asp.

4. "Junior High Bash Reaches Out to Younger Teens," *Arlington Catholic Herald*, June 17, 2004. See http://www.catholicherald.com/articles/04articles/bash0617.htm.

## Chapter 7: Patriotism

1. Peter Ustinov, *Quotable Ustinov* (Amherst, NY: Prometheus Books, 1995).

2. Personal e-mail interview, reproduced with permission.

3. Some opponents of open borders might use my mixed feelings to argue that immigrants pose a national security threat, especially in the war against terrorism. After 9/11/01, many Americans with South Asian or Middle Eastern roots felt like tattooing the American flag on our foreheads. We were eager to show loyalty to a country we love, but there was an undercurrent of fear that we might face harassment, mistrust, and even the possibility of internment or extradition. The Sikh community was in crisis, as some Americans vented their anger toward Osama Bin Laden against any man wearing a turban. The Japanese-American experience during World War II provided a cautionary example of what can happen in wartime to citizens who resemble the enemy.

4. Quoted in Peter Spiro, "Dual Nationality: Unobjectionable and Unstoppable," Center for Immigration Studies, July 2000. This paper was presented at the Cantigny Conference Series, Wheaton, Illinois.

5. Stanley Rensho, "Dual Citizenship and American National Identity," *Panel Discussion Transcript*, Center for Immigration Studies, National Press Club, Washington, DC, January 31, 2002.

6. "Dual Citizenship—Security Clearance Implications," U.S. Department of State, www.careers.state.gov/specialist/dual.html.

7. "Foreign Service Officers: FAQs," U.S. Department of State, www.careers .state.gov/officer/faqs.html.

8. Visit a few of the parenting links in the appendix of this book for some suggestions.

9. L. M. Montgomery, *Jane of Lantern Hill* (New York: Bantam, 1989), 8–9.

10. Ibid., 108–9.

11. Ibid., 147.

12. William of St. Thierry (1085–1148).

13. Guigo II, *The Ladder of Monks and Twelve Meditations* (Kalamazoo, MI: Cistercian, 1981).

14. "A divine read," www.homefaith.com/seasons/frame.html.

15. Janet Tashjian, *The Gospel According to Larry* (New York: Laurel Leaf, 2003).

16. Jonny Baker, "A Brand New Jesus," *Youthworker*, January/February 2001. See http://www.youthspecialties.com/articles/topics/culture/new_Jesus.php. Also online at http://jonnybaker.blogs.com/jonnybaker. Used by permission.

## Chapter 8: Savoir-Faire

1. http://www.zaadz.com/quotes/topics/diplomacy

2. *Encarta World English Dictionary*, Microsoft Corporation. Developed for Microsoft by Bloomsbury Publishing Plc., 1999.

3. Roger E. Axtell, *Do's and Taboos of Hosting International Visitors* (New York: Wiley, 1990), 1–2.

4. Dawn Mackeen, "Body Talk," *Salon*, November 19, 1998.

5. Andrew Greeley, "Ronstadt and Mellencamp: The Search for Roots," in *God in Popular Culture* (Chicago: Thomas More, 1998).

6. Leslie Wilson, Conversations with Scholars of American Popular Culture, Interview with Professor George Lipsitz, *Americana*, Spring 2002.

7. Bowling Green State University, http://www.bgsu.edu/departments/popc/bkgrnd.html.

8. Dawn Mackeen, "Body Talk," *Salon*, November 19, 1998.

9. Chuck Colson, "What Really Matters: Raising Helen," Breakpoint with Chuck Colson, May 28, 2004, http://www.pfm.org/Template.cfm?Section=Home&CONTENTID=12553&TEMPLATE=/ContentManagement/ContentDisplay.cfm.

10. Karl Gruber, "Common Denominators of Good Ambassadors," http://www.ediplomat.com.

11. T. M. Moore, *Redeeming Pop Culture: A Kingdom Approach* (Philipsburg, NJ: P & R, 2003), 35–36.

## Chapter 9: Tenacity

1. Herbert J. Muller, *Adlai E. Stevenson: A Study in Values* (New York: Harper & Row, 1967), 274.

2. Shawn Dorman, "New Hires and the Foreign Service," *Foreign Service Journal* (June 2004): 42.

3. Nicholas Kraler, "The Conduct of Diplomacy," *America's Other Army: Inside the Foreign Service*, Part 3, Special Reports, http://www.americandiplomacy.org.

4. Robert Burns, "I No Longer Want My MTV," *Magazine Americana*, February 2002. See http://www.americanpopularculture.com/archive/music/no_mtv.htm/. Reprinted by permission.

5. Peggy Blackford, "A Coup in Guinea-Bissau, 1998," *Foreign Service Journal* (February 2003): 33.

6. For more information, visit http://cci.gospelcom.net/ccihome/, Christian Camping International USA's online directory of 1,000-plus member organizations.

7. Wendell Berry, *Sabbaths* (New York: North Point Press, 1987), 88–89.

8. Tom Kagy, Asian American Media Watch, http://goldsea.com/Mediawatch/Moneymedia/moneymedia.html.

9. Leslie Wilson, "Bare-Naked Britney," *Magazine Americana*, February 2001. See http://www.american popularculture.com/archive/style/britney_spears.htm. Reprinted by permission.

10. Tim Madigan, "TV Shows and Video Games Teach Children to Kill, Psychologist Says," *Fort Worth Star-Telegram*, May 10, 1999, A18.

11. Bob Smithouser, "Isn't There a Better Way to Empower Women?" *Plugged In* 8 (11): 12. Used by permission.

## Chapter 10: Imagination

1. Nicholas Kraler, "The Conduct of Diplomacy," Special Report: "America's Other Army: Inside the Foreign Service," *Washington Times*, April 29, 2004.

2. Dan Murphy, "A consummate diplomat, indispensable to the UN," *Christian Science Monitor*, August 21, 2003.

3. Scholars believe the phrase "culture wars" comes from "Kulturkampf," a word coined in the 1870s when Otto von Bismarck sought to unite the German people in a struggle against "decadence."

4. Strickland Gillian, "The Reading Mother," *Best Loved Poems of the American People* (New York: Bantam Doubleday Dell, 1936), 376.

5. Ursula Le Guin, *The Language of the Night: Essays on Fantasy and Science Fiction* (New York: Putnam, 1979), 31.

6. G. K. Chesterton, "Fiction as Food," *The Spice of Life and Other Essays* (Beaconsfield, UK: Darwen Finlayson, 1964), 13.

7. David Elkind, *The Hurried Child: Growing Up Too Fast Too Soon* (Cambridge, MA: Perseus, 2001).

8. *Encarta World English Dictionary*, Microsoft Corporation. Developed for Microsoft by Bloomsbury Publishing Plc., 1999.

9. Janine Langan, "Imagination, Beauty, and Creativity," in *The Christian Imagination*, ed. Leland Ryken (New York: Waterbrook, 2002), 73.

10. Kate Kellaway, "A wizard with worlds," *The Observer*, October 22, 2000. See http://observer.guardian.co.uk/review/story/0,6903, 638058,00.html/

11. "Jedi 'religion' grows in Australia," BBC News, August 27, 2002. See http://news.bbc.co.uk/2/hi/entertainment/2218456.stm/

12. C. G. Jung, *The Archetypes and the Collective Unconscious*, vol. 9, pt. 1 of *The Collected Works of C. G. Jung*, 2nd ed., trans. R. F. C. Hull (Princeton, NJ: Princeton University Press, 1968), 155.

13. C. G. Jung, *Psychological Types*, vol. 6 of *The Collected Works of C. G. Jung*, trans. H. G. Baynes, rev. R. F. C. Hull (Princeton, NJ: Princeton University Press, 1971), 53.

14. Bruno Bettelheim, *The Uses of Enchantment: The Meaning and Importance of Fairy Tales* (New York: Vintage, 1989), 179.

15. Nadine Gordimer, "Writing and Being," 1991 Nobel Prize acceptance speech, *Nobel Lectures*, 1991–1995. See http://nobelprize.org/literature/laureates/1991/gordimer-lecture.html/.

16. Chris Monroe, "Interview with Todd Komarnicki," Christian Spotlight on the Movies, http://www.christiananswers.net/spotlight/movies/2003/komarnicki-todd.html.

17. Kristyn Komarnicki, personal e-mail interview, reproduced with permission.

18. Janine Langan, "Imagination, Beauty, and Creativity," in *The Christian Imagination*, ed. Leland Ryken (New York: Waterbrook, 2002), 65–66.

19. Peter Leithart, "Authors, Authority, and the Humble Reader," in *The Christian Imagination*, ed. Leland Ryken (New York: Waterbrook, 2002), 218–19.

20. C. S. Lewis, *Experiments in Criticism* (Cambridge, UK: Cambridge University Press, 1961).

21. Interview with Katherine Paterson, www.terabithia.com.

22. Madeleine L'Engle, *Walking on Water: Reflections on Faith and Art* (San Francisco: North Point, 1995).

# Acknowledgments

Thanks goes to my church, Newton Presbyterian Church, who asked me to teach a class on parenting; to Kristyn Komarnicki of *Prism* magazine, who printed an article I wrote based on the content in that class; and to Rodney Clapp, who saw the article and asked me to write this book. I'm grateful also to Rodney for his editorial direction and for Rebecca Cooper's work on the manuscript. Most of all, Rob and I are grateful to God for the privilege and high calling of parenting our sons, James and Timothy.